# More Recipes For SURFACES

# More Recipes For
# SURFACES

NEW AND EXCITING
IDEAS FOR
DECORATIVE PAINT
FINISHES

**Mindy Drucker and Nancy Rosen**

SIMON & SCHUSTER
AUSTRALIA

**To my parents, Shirley and Burton Drucker,**
with love and gratitiude
— M.D.

**To my daughter, Vanessa, my most beautiful creation,**
my most important accomplishment
— N.R.

More Recipes for Surfaces

First published in Australia in 1995 by
Simon and Schuster Australia
20 Barcoo Street East Roseville, NSW 2069

Viacom International
Sydney  New York  London  Toronto  Tokyo  Singapore

A Packaged Goods Incorporated Book

Conceived and produced by
Packaged Goods Incorporated
9 Murray Street, New York, NY 10007
A Quarto Company

Text by Mindy Drucker and Nancy Rosen
Design by Jan Melchior
Photographs by Mark Seelen
Illustrations by Erik Sheets
Découpage illustrations by Barbara Everard

© 1995 by Packaged Goods Incorporated

All rights reserved. No part of this publication may be reproduced, stored in a retrieval system, or transmitted, in any form or by any means, electronic, mechanical, photocopying, recording or otherwise, without the prior permission of the copyright holders.

National Library of Australia
Cataloguing in Publication Data

Drucker, Mindy.
More recipes for surfaces.

Bibliography.
Includes index.
ISBN 0 7318 0467 8

1. House painting - Amateurs, manuals. 2. Interior decoration - Amateurs, manuals. 3. Decoration and ornament - Amateurs, manuals. I. Rosen, Nancy, 1957- .

698.14

Colour Separations by Wellmak Printing Press Limited
Printed in Hong Kong by Midas Printing Limited

# ACKNOWLEDGMENTS

To my brothers-in-law, Mitchell Gold and Robert Williams, furniture makers whose designs and fabric choices, as well as insights into the way people live today, inspired my thinking. To the rest of my most patient and understanding family—Rhoda and Jack; Shirley and Burton; David, Alyssa, and Ilana; Chuck and Donna—always ready with a pep talk, devoted despite selfish (and lengthy) conversations about the creative process. And to the most patient and caring pair of all: my wonderful husband, Richard, who did his best and more to "keep the ship afloat"; and my darling daughter, Adrianne, an almost-three-year-old who never let me forget through the whole writing process that being "mommy" means most.

— M.D.

Special thanks to Melissa Merendino and Rob O'Connor. In addition to running their own contracting businesses, they make time to work and teach with me in my studio in Maplewood, New Jersey. To my lifelong friend Francine Rothschild, who introduced me to decorative painting along with a lot of other great things in life. Creativity grows best with experimentation, shared ideas and encouragement. I am lucky to be surrounded by people who have helped to make this all so much fun. Thanks Mr. Wilson, Love Dennis.

—N.R.

Nancy and Mindy would also like to extend special thanks to the following people and companies: interior designer Jeffrey Brooks, of Oldwick, NJ, for bringing writer and painter together; photographer Mark Seelen for working so diligently to present the recipes in the clearest possible light, as well as for being so wonderful to work with; Melissa Merendino, accomplished fine artist and decorative painter, of Norwalk, CT, for brainstorming and assisting with painting for the project; muralist Nick Devlin, of Tewksbury, NJ, and Jeffrey Brooks, for allowing us to include a fine example of decorative painting, the designer showhouse room with which Nancy assisted them, in these pages; master painter Rob O'Connor, of Milburn, NJ, for his insights into painting interiors and furniture; Steve Marcketta, of Suburban Paint, Milburn, NJ, for his expert work on the paint formulas provided in this book; to Werner Meier of Design Impressions Gallery of Short Hills and Wall, NJ, for contributing fabric used in the book; Kevin Kelly of Structural Arts for his connections; Jan Melchior, for her great book design; Anne Newgarden for her careful copy editing; Marta Hallett, Kristen Schilo, Margaux King, and Tatiana Ginsberg of Packaged Goods Inc., for their help in bringing this book to life.

Packaged Goods Inc. would like to thank Dominic Berretto, Angie Hice, Jim Naughton, and Barry Silverman at Home Depot for their contribution of time, materials, and support. We also thank Allen Shefts at Pearl Paint/Pearl Art and Crafts stores for his generous donation to this project.

# CONTENTS

FOREWORD **How to Use this Book** 8

## PART ONE
## GENERAL INFORMATION 10

INTRODUCTION **What Decorative Painting Can Do For You** 12

CHAPTER ONE **Colour: The Flavour in Every Recipe** 16

CHAPTER TWO **Paints and Tools: The Basics** 24

CHAPTER THREE **Preparing to Paint** 38

CHAPTER FOUR **Mixing Paints** 58

CHAPTER FIVE **Before You Begin** 64

## PART TWO
## THE RECIPES 72

CHAPTER SIX **Metals** 74

Technique 1: Copper Verdigris—78
Technique 2: Bronze Verdigris—80
Technique 3: Rusted Metal—82

CHAPTER SEVEN **Stone** 84

Technique 1: Flagstone—87
Technique 2: Stone-work—90
Technique 3: Granite—92
Technique 4: Malachite—96

CHAPTER EIGHT **"Fantasy" Marbling** 100

Technique 1: Red Marble—103
Technique 2: Blue Marble—106
Technique 3: Sedimentary-Style Marble—110

CHAPTER NINE **Reasonable Replicas** 114

Technique 1: Fresco—117
Technique 2: Leather—119
Technique 3: Stucco—121
Technique 4: Cloudy Sky—124
Technique 5: Brick—126
Technique 6: Moiré—130

CHAPTER TEN **"Textured" Wall Finishes** 134

Technique 1: Feather-Duster Finish—137
Technique 2: Corduroy Ragging On—139
Technique 3: Corduroy Ragging Off—141
Technique 4: Plastic-Wrap Ragging Off—144
Technique 5: Plastic Bag Ragging Off—146
Technique 6: Spattering in Four Colours—148
Variation: Blue Spatter Finish—150
Technique 7: Flogging—151

CHAPTER ELEVEN
**Small-Surface Specialties and Stencilling** 154

Technique 1: Crackle Glaze—157
Technique 2: Découpage—160
Technique 3: Transferring and Cutting a Stencil
from Cardboard—165
Technique 4: Transferring and Cutting a Stencil
from Acetate—165
Technique 5: Tile—166
Technique 6: Grape-Leaf Motif—168
Technique 7: Leopard Skin—172
Technique 8: Architectural Moulding—174
Tile Stencil—178
Grape-Leaf Motif Stencil—179
Leopard Skin Stencil—180
Architectural Moulding Stencil—181-182
Sources—183
Index—185
For Further Reading—189

# FOREWORD
## How to Use this Book

All the information you need to create more than 30 decorative paint finishes in the latest colours is right in your hands, in a format specially designed to make the process as easy as possible. Just think of this how-to guide as a cookbook, and the painted finishes as chef d'oeuvres that, with a little practise, are well within your creative grasp.

Decorative painting and cooking have a lot in common. Both have basic recipes and procedures—in cooking, how to prepare a pie crust, make a sauce, design a menu; in painting, how to prepare a surface, mix a glaze, plan a colour scheme.

Like the first edition of *Recipes for Surfaces*, the new edition of *More Recipes for Surfaces* has been modeled after a good cookbook. At the heart of the book are the detailed "recipes" for creating each finish. These step-by-step guides show photos of each crucial step, as well as the finished effect and, where appropriate, the natural material that inspired the finish in the first place.

Each recipe is self-contained; you'll find a "recipe card" listing all the tools needed: what surfaces a finish particularly suits; how many people can most easily execute it; whether you must varnish the finish; and squares of colour showing each paint colour that has gone into creating the final effect. In addition, the introduction to each recipe discusses decorating styles it works well with, other tools you can use in creating it, additional colour suggestions in which to execute it, tips for making the job simpler, and more.

Although geared to beginners, the book offers a range of recipes, identified by degree of difficulty on their recipe cards using paint-tin symbols ( ). The simplest recipes feature one paint tin; the most challenging, three paint tins.

Even the most challenging recipes are probably within your reach. To ensure success, read the whole recipe before you begin, as well as the introduction to the chapter. Review the general information in Part One of the book on colour, tools, paints, surface preparation, and more.

Then prepare samples. Test your colours and patterns on large pieces of illustration board from art shops, studying them in the light of the room in which the effects will be seen at several different times of day. (Colours change with the light: a pleasing blue in morning sunlight might turn dull grey at dusk.) See Chapter Five, *Before You Begin,* for more on making samples.

Some techniques, such as marbling, combine several skills, from simple sponging to freehand painting. Don't be distressed if abstract versions are all you can master at first. In fact, this more casual style is often better suited to today's decorating styles. Of course, if you have your heart set on lifelike marble, you may want to hire a professional decorative painter and use the ideas in this book to convey to her the look you want.

One thing you won't find in this book are shots of elaborate interiors. This is done to help eliminate distractions and encourage you to study the techniques for themselves. It can be hard to focus on a finish in a room full of furnishings, flooring, and fabrics. And it can be hard to tell if a colour in a photo of a room might suit your space because of the great variations in light that might exist between that room and yours.

For that same reason, most of the techniques in this book have been executed on pieces of plasterboard under the same lighting conditions. Once you learn the techniques, you can decide how best to adapt them to your particular spaces.

For those of you who have the first edition, *Recipes for Surfaces*, please note that even a cursory comparison to *More Recipes for Surfaces* will turn up numerous variations—the size of a cloth used to "rag" a surface, the kind of paint brush used to apply glaze, the way paint is mixed. As an eyewitness to the working methods of two different decorative painters who produced the finishes for these two books, I can report that both ways work extremely well.

What you'll find in *More Recipes for Surfaces* are the suggested paint colours, brush types, rag sizes, and everything else Nancy used to create the finishes shown here. But there is a clear and valuable lesson in the variations between the two books: you don't need to get hung up on the tyranny of only painting a certain way. You can substitute one tool for another. You can change the colours of a glaze. And you'll still get great results. In fact, you'll get a finish truly your own as well as a good understanding of how to execute the technique for future projects—all without the unnecessary angst involved in trying to create an exact replica.

What Nancy most wanted to share in *More Recipes for Surfaces* is how easy and fun decorative painting can be—that, while steeped in tradition and technique, it also makes a simple, affordable, and attractive way to decorate your home today. To that end, everything in this book has been simplified as much as possible, often based on her experience teaching adult-education courses in decorative painting, so that you can get great results fast, with minimal fuss.

Look closely and you'll realise that many of the finishes you see in this book are the ones you see all the time in magazines and stores, often at hefty prices. The colours are from the latest decorating schemes, the ones that colour experts think will dominate in coming years. Go into any department store and you'll find bed linens, lamp shades, picture frames, and even already-decorative-painted furnishings in the same colours as the finishes you see here. Using these "colour suggestions", you can easily get a coordinated decorator look for your home. Or, if your walls are white and your furniture is inherited, you can use these finishes to update your interiors in the latest colours and "textured" looks.

Don't forget, however, that all this explaining on our part doesn't mean you can just dive right in. *You must practise before starting on your surfaces.* In fact, you'll see reminders to practise throughout the book. Take it from one relative novice to another: this is the key to success with decorative painting.

— Mindy Drucker

# Part One

# GENERAL INFORMATION

# INTRODUCTION
## WHAT DECORATIVE PAINTING CAN DO FOR YOU

**A painted finish can serve many functions. Here, a "spattered" wall subtly introduces a host of colours, helps link the surfaces of the room, and makes a unique statement.**

Decorative painting is everywhere you look these days, and its popularity is a real plus for do-it-yourselfers. How-to guides like this one have made "trade secrets" of this age-old art public. Paint, glaze, and art supply manufacturers have made the tools more widely available.

Along with a stronger presence on the interior design scene has come a looser, more casual approach to decorative painting. Classics such as marbling, graining, stencilling, sponging, ragging, and spattering still get a lot of play. But, as you'll see in this book, decorative painting also includes "printing" with tools as diverse as a feather duster or paint scraper.

Even the definition of decorative painting has been expanded. Traditionally, it means applying two layers of interior house paint (the base coat) and then topping them with a transparent paint layer called glaze. Because the glaze never fully covers the base coat, thus allowing some of the colour beneath to show through, your eye does some mixing of its own right on the surface, creating a rich hue with a sense of depth.

In some cases, the process is even easier; instead of glaze, the top layer is simply opaque paint. Because of the way in which it is applied, the top paint layer still never fully covers the base coat, causing a similar mixing by the eye.

A host of reasons account for the recent popularity of decorative painting: its ability to serve as a more affordable stand-in for wallpaper; the way it can transform a junk shop find into a treasure; the diversity of colour it can create. But perhaps the biggest reason is the way it can coordinate with so many of the latest decorating trends. It is amazing and wonderful that you can transform your home, or just certain rooms, into brand new living spaces.

## ADDING TEXTURE

A good example of this is how these finishes can add "texture" to a room—or, more accurately, the *impression* of texture. By applying glaze or paint with tools, from sponges to rags to combs, rollers, and brushes, you create flat patterns that the eye interprets as texture, a welcome addition to many looks.

Texture is central to a monochromatic colour scheme. Picture the classic all-white interior. Where does the design interest come from? A subtle blend of tones and textures: off-white linen lining the walls, gauzy white draperies at the windows, crisp white canvas slipcovers on the furniture, warm white crewelwork rug underfoot.

Texture is also in keeping with the trend toward eclecticism, mixing and matching materials within a room. For example, in a dining room, instead of a matched set, you might find a glass table ringed by upholstered chairs and paired with wood cabinetry. Surfaces in a decorative finish can hold their own in such a mix.

The same can be said of decorative painting with "global", or "ethnic", design styles; the "texture" of painted finishes can help balance strong elements in a room. In Chapter Ten, *"Textured" Wall Finishes,* you'll find several easily attainable decorative effects that would fit the bill.

## INJECTING COLOUR

Another way decorative painting fits today's styles is through colour. Colour is the heart of decorative painting. It is by picking the right colours that you'll be able to recreate many of the decorative-painting looks you see in stores and magazines today.

There are several ways to do this. The colours in this book were developed with an eye toward reflecting the latest styles seen in decorating magazines, catalogues, and stores, and were chosen based on the latest research into the colour trends most likely to prevail over the next five years and beyond.

Note, however, that the colours suggested here are meant only to give you an idea of what's "fashionable" and what's coming. You must combine this information with your personal taste, the furnishings you have and those you plan to buy, as well as where and how you live, to come up with the colours and styles of decorative painting that are right for you. The power of decorative painting lies in its easily attainable ability to make your decor unique. Don't be a slave to either fashion or "expert opinion". Nobody knows better than you what you'll be happy living with.

## CONVEYING STYLES

As you'll find in Chapter One, colour can perform many functions, from giving rooms a restful or lively ambience to making a space seem larger or cosier than its size.

Colour can also help you express decorating styles. Following are four colour palettes from which the colours in this book were selected. Loosely, they represent four very broad decorating styles or sensibilities with which you can imbue a room.

However, keep in mind that there is much crossover among the colour groups, and that colour *combinations* are a major part of what makes an interior colour scheme work. The neutral palette could easily accept accents from any of the other groups. A fresco-pastel might make the perfect glaze over a base coat in a deep jewel tone.

In addition, colours from each group are used in varying intensities and val-

**GENERAL INFORMATION**

ues—i.e., a modern bright colour toned down with grey or white. They have also been used in varying quantities, thus greatly altering their impact. To get a certain look, you won't use all the colours in a group at once; nor will you be using them in the same quantities within your space. That's why two strong colours that look like they would never "match up" may actually work beautifully together when one is on the walls, the other is used as an accent, and there are soothing neutrals between them. The finished effect is astonishing.

**Using neutral hues in stencilling helps you couple natural colours with innovative designs.**

## NEUTRALS

The biggest colour story is the move to a more natural colour palette. Perhaps part of the rising tide of environmentalism, the new neutrals are more reminiscent of earth tones, going beyond beiges and greys into yellows and greens. Sophisticated and subdued, they are beautifully served through decorative painting's layered effect.

In decorative painting, these tones help you recreate natural materials such as leather, stucco, and stone. They can be great backdrops for the fine wood furniture of Modern design as well as the wide-ranging collectibles of Country style.

They are also good foils for the trappings of "global" style, which can include a broad array of multicultural influences from our own country and the world beyond. They blend with the natural materials of the style—sisal, rattan, tortoiseshell, mahogany—and provide a framework for the strong patterns, often in the form of batiklike fabrics in rich hues, that are one of its hallmarks. Neutrals are easy to live with and complement many styles.

## FRESCO-INSPIRED PASTELS

Pale violet, sage green, dusty rose—these soft, yet rich and warm, colours inspired by fresco painting are the new pastels. Toned down, they tie in well with neutrals to create finishes with complex colouring and great depth. These greyer, dustier pastels have a comfortable, casual, well-worn feel, like that of faded floral slipcovers or a favourite old cotton shirt.

You can match them comfortably with decors as diverse as Santa Fe and Victorian, the latter, incidentally, a period in which decorative painting flourished. They are also the colours of rich yet subtle Pompeii-inspired interiors. You can see decorative-painting examples of this colour palette in the "Sedimentary-Style Marble" finish, the "Fresco" finish, and the "Stencilled Tile" effect.

INTRODUCTION

## MODERN BRIGHT COLOURS

One important influence on colour trends is technology. Today, manufacturers of many materials for the home, from fabrics to flooring, can use technology to create brighter colours more easily than ever before. This has brought new freedom in creating coordinated decorating schemes with modern bright colours, a palette of hues reprised from the 1950s.

Daring shades of lime and lemon, salmon, coral, and periwinkle can help create lively interiors with a contemporary air. Yet, they can be relaxed, too, bringing to mind the casual feel of island living. This versatility makes bright hues an exciting option.

Combinations of these colours aren't as shocking as they might first seem. You find them together often in nature; because they work so well, you may not have stopped to think about it. They work because they have similar colour intensity, a characteristic that creates a balance among them—no one strong hue dominates and draws the eye. (For more on colour characteristics, see Chapter One, *Colour: The Flavour in Every Recipe*.)

Many of these brights seem to have come straight out of a country cottage garden; they can often be found in the Laura Ashley-type floral prints typical of the country cottage style. These days, even more than the hues of blooms, the colour emphasis is on the greens of the garden's foliage.

A single bright hue teamed with white or a neutral can make a striking statement either in a room or when combined in a decorative effect. See, for instance, the "Feather-Duster Finish", or the "Blue Marble" technique.

## JEWEL TONES

These dark colours make strong statements in a room setting. They are the colours of the gentlemen's club or of the great country houses. Jewel tones are also great accent colours—witness the strength of sapphire, ruby, and emerald glass pieces in a natural decor. They convey opulence and formality, tying together rooms filled with classic luxuries: gilt mirrors, velvet sofas, and tassled pillows, and marble statuary.

**Jewel tones draw the eye to the surface they adorn. Used simply they enhance, not overwhelm.**

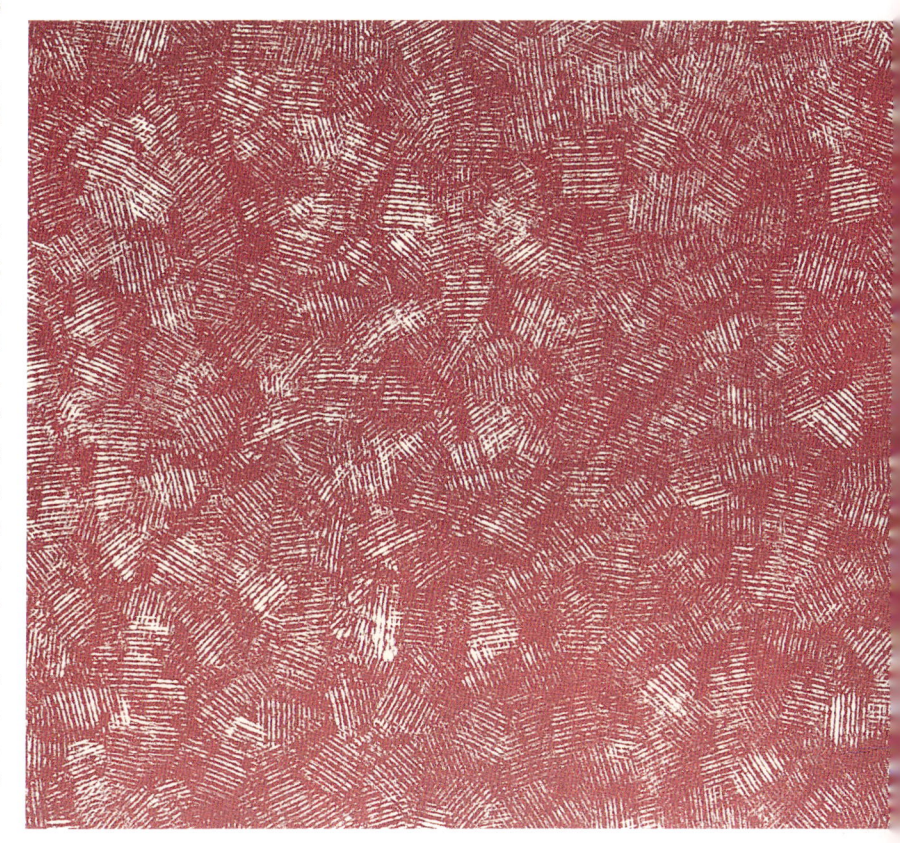

In decorative painting, jewel tones make great base-coat colours, seen peeking through a light-coloured glaze—see, for example, the richly coloured surface you can create with the "Corduroy Ragging On" technique. The jewel tones are also perfect complements to metallic finishes, such as those you'll find in Chapter Six, *Metals*.

**GENERAL INFORMATION**

# CHAPTER ONE

# COLOUR: THE FLAVOUR IN EVERY RECIPE

Sweet success with decorative painting comes from a mix of many ingredients, but none is more important than colour. It's easy to see why. Colour can transform the character of a finish, taking it from subtle to bold, traditional to contemporary, formal to casual.

In the Introduction to this book, there are a host of ideas on how to use painted finishes with today's most popular decorating styles. The key to doing this is knowing which hues can help you capture the look and feel of a style.

That's how the colours for the finishes in this book were chosen—based on current design trends. In these pages, you can find the same looks you love in stores and magazines, and then use the colour suggestions and guidance supplied to achieve these looks much more affordably.

**In deep, rich blue, this finish resembles luxurious Chinese water silk. But, if done in soft browns, it could easily take on the look of folk-art style wood.**

Don't forget that you can also use the "mix-and-match" principle: maybe a finish you like isn't shown in colours that suit your decor; but another finish is. You can take the colour suggestions for the other finish to the paint store, and have its colours made up for you. Be sure, however, to follow "paint-system" and "paint-consistency" requirements for the recipe you'll execute. (For more on paint systems and consistency, see Chapter Two, *Paints and Tools*.)

There is, of course, no reason to limit yourself to colours pictured here. In fact, the best way to think of all the recipes is as "serving suggestions", much like the recipes you might find on a packet of pasta. There are so many variations; we have only scratched the surface of the great array of colours and patterns decorative painting makes available to us.

Sometimes, so much choice can be a little unnerving. You're probably well acquainted with the challenge it can be just to pick standard paint colours for a room—coordinating with elements already in place, dealing with the pressure of knowing you'll have to live with your choice for some time. And even if you narrow your options to safe-and-neutral white, there are all the subtle shades that fall under that heading.

With decorative painting, it can be even more challenging. You must pick more than one colour for each surface and make sure that those colours work well together.

To better your odds of successful selection—whether you plan to buy your paint and glaze ready-mixed or mix them yourself—it pays to know something about colour: the way colours work together, the interior design rules governing them, even how they influence the way you feel. The best place to begin is with a look at the concepts known as "colour theory" and how they work in interior design.

## UNDERSTANDING COLOUR

**W**hen it comes to identifying pleasing colour schemes, our earliest paint-box lessons still apply: any hue can be made by combining the three primary colours—red, yellow, and blue—with varying amounts of black and white. By mixing pairs of primaries, you form the three secondary colours: red and yellow make orange; yellow and blue make green; blue and red make violet. Then, by blending the secondaries, you get the tertiaries: olive, for one, which comes from mixing green with violet.

Today, however, thanks to technology, we should probably qualify the basic rule to say that *almost* any colour can be created from the primaries. In reality, the more colours you combine, the less vibrant your result will be; so manufacturers now produce a wide range of colours whose brilliance would be hard to match by starting with the primaries.

**Strong colours combined with a striking pattern make this effect, done simply with a feather duster, a real eye-catcher.**

COLOUR: THE FLAVOUR IN EVERY RECIPE

## COLOUR HARMONY

**T**o grasp the relationships among colours, you can use the colour wheel, pictured here. Like the face of a clock, it has 12 parts. You'll find the primary colours at 12 o'clock (yellow), four o'clock (red), and eight o'clock (blue). The secondary colours are at two o'clock (orange), six o'clock (violet), and 10 o'clock (green). In the remaining six spaces are the intermediate colours, so called because they lie between the primary and secondary colours.

From the position of colours on the wheel, you can identify harmonious blends. Among recommended combinations are *similar* colours, such as orange and yellow, which appear near each other on the wheel. Other options are *complementary* colours, such as red and green, which appear opposite each other. Complementaries serve a special purpose in decorating: they tone each other down to help balance a scheme.

A colour also blends well with the colours flanking its complementary—orange with either blue-green or blue-violet, for instance. This arrangement is called *split-complementary*.

You'll also discover that *triads*—any three colours equidistant on the wheel (the primaries, for example)—will harmonize.

**You can use a colour wheel to get a feel for how colours work together. Keep in mind that colours on the wheel are in "pure" form; but the same principles apply to all their different values and intensities—i.e., pale pink would occupy the same space on the wheel as red.**

**GENERAL INFORMATION**

## COLOUR CHARACTERISTICS

Even though the categories mentioned might be unfamiliar to you, you'll probably find many of your favourite combinations fit into them naturally. You may not recognize them at first, however, because on the colour wheel they are in "pure" form, and this isn't often the form in which they are used in decorating, of course.

A colour has three main characteristics: its *hue*, the colour family to which it belongs; its *intensity*, how dull or vivid it is; and its *value*, how dark or light it is. By varying the intensity and value of pure colour, we derive a multitude of others.

For example, by altering the value of pure red, we can get both rose and pink, which belong to the same colour family and, thus, share the same position on the colour wheel. To change the value of a colour, you mix black and/or white into it. Mixing in white creates a *tint*; adding black gives a *shade*; blending in grey makes a *tone*.

## CLASSIC COLOUR SCHEMES

Based on these principles, we can devise colour schemes that are pleasing and easily achieved. Using different values of the same colour—cream, taupe, and deep brown, for instance—will give you a monochromatic arrangement. The scheme can be enhanced by decorative painting's two-tone effect. Try taupe walls sponge-painted over with cream glaze to add subtle design interest to a subdued setting. Sometimes, the simplest schemes provide a dramatic effect.

You can also create a harmonious setting with different colours that have the same value: three deep jewel tones, for example. The contrast between, say, a rich red, gold, and green brings vibrancy to the scene, while the similarity in values ties them together and prevents one colour from dominating and throwing the scheme off balance.

Because you may not be used to thinking of colours in terms of their value, identifying different colours with the same value may take some practice. To get a feel for values, imagine looking at a black-and-white photo of a room of your house. Or, even better, take an actual black-and-white photo of it. In the photo, all the colours in the room that have the same value will be the same shade of grey. By diminishing the obvious differences in hues, you can more easily spot those of similar value. (You may also be able to get a sense of similar values by looking at a room and half-closing your eyes.)

Keep in mind that simplicity can be trusted when it comes to colour schemes. Consider using just a range of neutrals—whites, beiges, greys. A subtle scheme like that makes a fine showcase for intricate painted finishes that might look busy or take a back seat in a more intensely coloured setting.

Another option is to link your favourite hue with white or a pale neutral. In fact, using your preferred colour as an accent will produce a scheme that is notable for its flexibility. As styles or your tastes change, you can just switch the accent colour to give your neutral scheme a new look. Choosing a light accent colour that contrasts less with your pale neutral background is a great way to give your interior a calming, relaxed air. Remember, too, that some of the most pleasing colour combinations—and, some of the most unexpected—occur in nature; so keep your eyes open for inspiration.

## CREATING A COLOUR SCHEME

Interior designers have many methods for developing colour schemes. A simple and effective one is to select the curtain or upholstery fabric first, and then create a custom look by matching walls, floors, and furnishings in coordinating hues.

If you're going to be mixing your own paints, picking your fabric beforehand is a safer bet. You can undoubtedly create a hue to match your fabric, but you might not as easily find a fabric to go with a distinctive colour you've specially blended. If you'll be using premixed paints, you'll probably be safe picking your paint colour first. The colours chosen for the finishes here were specially devised to coordinate with many of today's most popular decorating styles and home furnishings.

When decorating a room based on a fabric, professionals often advise that the background colour of a print fabric and the base coat of your walls be the same colour. Then you can "pull out" other hues in the fabric pattern for coordinated accents; for a more sophisticated effect, you might want to skip the hue that appears in largest quantities in the pattern and bring out other colours instead.

Another method is to select three colours you like and apply them in varying quantities. Make one colour dominant. Use the second colour about half as much, and include the third as an accent.

A third way is to base your colour scheme on a favorite object—a painting, a piece of pottery, an antique chair, a kilim rug. Its colours don't have to be the main ones in your room. You can create a neutral backdrop, then use the colours in your object as an accent.

## COLOUR CAN CREATE MOODS

Don't underestimate the power of colour to establish a tone for your interiors. After a long day at the office, do you want to come home to a cool, peaceful oasis? Colour can arrange it. Do you live in a space that gets little light, but long for a bright, eye-opening spot? Colour can create that too.

Colour can give your home a single all-over ambience or let you change the look from room to room. For instance, use soft hues that create a relaxed look for private spaces like bedrooms, then turn to deeper, more formal colours for areas in which you entertain.

## COLOURS HAVE TEMPERATURE

Red and yellow aren't the only "warm" colours; nor are blue and green the only "cool" ones. There are "warm" and "cool" versions of all colours. It depends on what other hues a colour contains. Green with more blue in it will seem "cooler" than a green with more yellow.

Often, "more" might be just a few drops of a cool or warm colour. Nowhere can this be better seen than in the great variety of "white" paints. Cool whites have the slightest bluish or purplish cast, while warm whites might carry a tinge of pink, yellow, red, or orange.

These little differences in quantity can make a big difference in the way a colour is perceived in a room. For instance, warm whites appear to advance, while cool whites seem to recede.

Many people seem to favor warm whites for their living spaces, but cool whites also have a place. While a warm white might be welcome in a room that gets little sun, a cool one can be appreciated in a space consumed with warmth.

**GENERAL INFORMATION**

## COLOUR TRANSFORMS SPACES

Besides imparting your personal stamp and establishing a mood, colour can alter a room visually. Consider these questions to determine the kind of "colour therapy" you need for each room you are planning to paint. *What size is the room?* Painting a room a light colour will make it appear larger; applying a dark hue will give it a cosy feel. *What do you want the focus of the room to be—walls, woodwork, flooring, furnishings?* Varying the intensity of colours —that is, combining light or vivid hues with dark or dull ones—lets you place the emphasis where you want it. *What is the room used for, and how often is it used?* A hallway might be better suited to an especially stimulating colour scheme

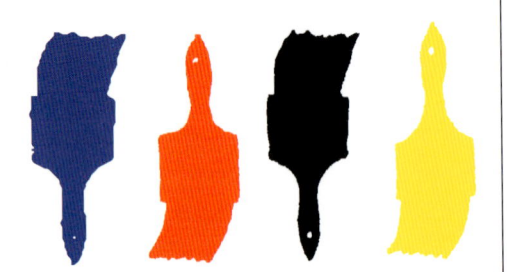

**Light colours.** Whatever hue you choose, light tints of it will give you a soft look. This easy-to-live-with quality makes light colours favourites in decorating, especially when enlivened with accents in a brighter or darker hue.

**Bright colours.** Even more exuberant than the warm colours, the brights include shades of blue, yellow, black, white, and red. They have a contemporary flavour, but even in children's rooms, we rarely see even two together. In groups, they can overwhelm.

**Dark colours.** Black and other dark hues are less frequent choices for large areas of interiors. Jewel-tone colours, such as deep red, purple, green, and blue, have historical associations and a more formal air. These hues can be just right for the walls of a formal dining room or living room. But they more often serve as rich accents.

**Dull colours.** Shades of grey mellow the dull hues, which are said to help lower stress and bring on a contemplative mood. To keep them from seeming too vague, link them with bright accents. Experiment to discover the new options these hues can offer as part of a two-tone colour scheme.

COLOUR: THE FLAVOUR IN EVERY RECIPE

because you pass through it, rather than spend a lot of time there. *What are the colour preferences of those who will be useing the room most?* For happiest results, review your choices with those who share the room. *Which direction does the room face?* A room that is exposed to a cooler light might best be served by bright colours. *How much natural and artificial light does the room get?* Prepare samples and see how they look in the most common lighting conditions that occur in the room. Examine how they look at different times of day. *Will spaces adjacent to the room also display painted finishes?* If you can see one room from another, you might link their colour schemes by employing a common hue—the main colour in one room could be an accent in the next, for example.

**Cool colours.** Cool hues, including blue, violet, grey, and green, give a feeling of calm. Perhaps their "coolness" stems from their association with water. This coolness has contributed to their popularity in hot climates. Be aware that some cool colours contain red, and can appear warm.

**Natural colours.** Subtle and complex, natural hues can be soothing. In their simplicity, they provide a rich look. They can be pale, clear, dark, muted, or bright and are generally blends of many hues. To spice up dark or muted colours complement them with a bright hue also found in nature.

**Warm colours.** Ranging from red to yellow, these splashy hues demand attention, lend excitement, and "heat up" even a small, dark room. Psychologists speculate they may increase our drive and help us work faster, making them good choices for a kitchen or home office. When combined with cool colours, they always dominate.

**Surprising colours.** Rarely found in nature or teamed in daily life, they get our attention. Among them are hues contrary to their natural brightness—dull orange, for instance—combinations with less contrast, such as magenta and purple. Note: colours in this category that once seemed startling have become conventional with use.

GENERAL INFORMATION

CHAPTER TWO

PAINTS AND
TOOLS:
THE BASICS

Before you head out to the paint shop, you have a decision to make: will you use water- or oil-based paints? Just about all paints are composed of three elements: *pigment*, powder ground from natural or synthetic materials that give paint its colour; *binder*, the vehicle that carries and fixes pigment and then dries to a protective film; and *thinners*: the solvents that dilute paint to a workable consistency. The differences between water- and oil-based paints lie in their binders and thinners. For water-based paints, such as emulsion or acrylics, the binder is acrylic resin, and the thinner is water. For oil-based paints, the binder is usually linseed oil, and the solvent is white spirit.

# PAINTS

BASE YOUR WATER/OIL DECISION ON THESE FACTORS:

*The finish you plan to execute.* For a guiding hand in this area, turn to the recipe card in Part Two of this book for the finish you've selected to see which type of paint is recommended.

*The surface you will paint on.* Are you planning to paint the walls of your brand new home or spruce up some second-hand painted furniture? Are you going to rejuvenate a rusty old garden gate? See the chart at the end of Chapter Three, *Preparing to Paint*, for advice on the type of paint that will work best for your particular surface.

*Also consider the pros and cons of each paint type:*

## OIL-BASED PAINTS

**The Pros**
- traditional medium for decorative painting that is particularly suited to advanced techniques such as wood graining
- a boon to the novice painter, especially in executing a more challenging finish, because oils dry more slowly and, thus, allow more time to work and fix mistakes
- dries to an especially durable finish that is well suited to areas that see heavy traffic or objects that get a lot of that "human touch"—like a hall floor, kitchen chairs, or skirting board and wall mouldings that you might find yourself banging into with a vacuum cleaner on a regular basis

**The Cons**
- slower drying time means the project will take longer because you have to wait longer before recoating a surface
- clean up takes longer than with water-based paints, and less-environmentally safe solvents need to be used
- safety precautions need to be taken because oils give off fumes and are flammable

## WATER-BASED PAINTS

**The Pros**
- faster drying time—a plus when you need to apply several layers because you wait less time between coats
- easier to clean up—just requires water
- safer for you—they don't give off fumes
- safer for the environment—they are thinnned with water and don't contain solvents

**The Cons**
- faster drying time—a problem when you're first learning a technique and need extra time to get it right; if you're working on a very large surface; or if you're trying to execute a "subtractive" technique (see Chapter Five, *Before You Begin*), generally considered a "two-person" job, with just one person. Suggestions for slowing drying times appear later in this chapter; but, depending on the technique, they may not be enough to allow successful execution in water-based paints.

Also note that although water-based paints like emulsion and acrylic are easily cleaned up when wet, they are permanent and water-resistant once dry. Drips and splashes are hard to wipe up. Remove them with methylated spirits.

26  PAINTS AND TOOLS: THE BASICS

# Choosing a Paint System

Remember that you're not just selecting the kind of paint for your finish coat—you're selecting a paint system. For a strong, durable finish, your best bet is usually to use the same paint type throughout your project—from primer to base coat to glaze.

This is especially true if you're using an oil system. A water-based acrylic glaze won't "take" over an oil-based undercoat; the glaze tends to bead and can chip and crack. (This is actually the basis for the "Crackle Glaze" recipe in Chapter Eleven).

There is one major exception to the paint-system rule that many people will appreciate: *you can paint oil over emulsion.* If your home is under 25 years old, your painted walls are most likely emulsion Thus, if those walls have a good nonporous emulsion base in an appropriate colour (paint must be silk finish or gloss to be nonporous), and you want to do a finish best executed in oils over them, go ahead. (Just prepare the walls as explained in the chart in Chapter Three.) Or, if you want to change the base colour, you can still recoat with emulsion even if you plan to do your decorative finish in oils. The reason this is possible is that water-based paints dry quickly and fully, creating a surface that won't repel oil.

If your walls have been painted with oil-based paint, and you want to repaint them with emulsion, you will need to apply a special primer first; see your paint or DIY store for recommendations. To learn more about the compatibility of base coats and primers, see Chapter Three, *Preparing to Paint*. See the following sections for the kinds of paints to buy.

## WATER SYSTEM

### BASE COAT

Buy emulsion for your base coat. Emulsion is the base coat for all the finishes in this book, whether the glaze layer uses water-based paint or oil.

Emulsion comes in two main finishes: matt and silk (eggshell and gloss are also available). For most of the finishes in this book, the base coat is silk.

In some cases, your choice will depend on the character of the finish. For example, anything that adds more sheen to faux marble might be welcome; but a faux-flagstone wall might look a little more natural with a matt base.

Note, however, that if you are using a "subtractive" technique, in which you apply and then remove glaze or paint, you may be best off with a silk base coat because it is less absorbent. To choose your base coat colour, see Chapter Four, *Mixing Paints*. For the correct primer, see Chapter Three, *Preparing to Paint*.

As we learn more about the effects of solvents on the environment, more and more paint manufacturers are responding by developing a wider range of water-based paint products. However, even water-based paints contain chemicals, and no paint should ever be disposed of by simply being poured down the drain.

### GLAZE

Water-based glaze is mainly water (60 to 80 per cent), which you combine with colour in the form of water-based paints and acrylic medium, a transparent gel available under many different brand names in art stores and craft shops. Acrylic medium comes in matt and silk finishes. Water-based glazes in a limited selection of colours are also available premixed in art stores, DIY centres, and by mail.

In this book, with the exception of a special premixed crackle glaze in one recipe, no actual *water-based* glazes were used—a glaze being defined by its transparent quality derived from a glazing medium. The top coats on the water-based finishes are emulsion or acrylic paint, either straight from the can or diluted with varying amounts of water. On the recipe cards for those finishes, instead of a "Glaze" colour, you'll find an "Applied Finish" colour. (The oil-based finish coats, on the other hand, are for the most part actual transparent "glazes", made with oil-based glazing liquid.)

**A close-up of a wooden chair reveals its "aged" finish. The effect was simple to achieve with the help of a special premixed crackle-glazing product.**

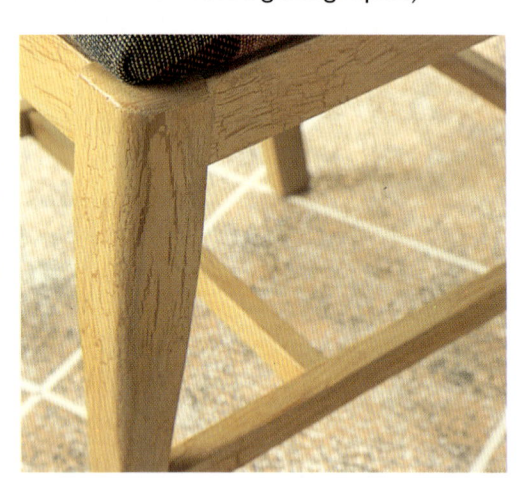

This way of doing things contributes to the ease with which many of the finishes in this book can be accomplished. It also greatly shortens preparation time, eliminating glaze-mixing steps. Using paints instead of glazes does move the finished effects away from the transparency of traditional decorative painting. But, as the photos show, it can produce beautiful results all its own. You still get "depth" and softness by applying just a little bit of paint lightly in layers and by using tools whose "broken" impressions let the previous layers show through.

For thinning water-based paints and for cleaning brushes, use water. To find out how to get the glaze colour you want turn to Chapter Four, *Mixing Paints*.

# OIL SYSTEM

## BASE COAT

Today's oil-based interior house paints are composed of a mix of oil and resin that dries faster and contains no lead. Oil-based paint comes in flat, eggshell, silk, and gloss finishes. Flat oil-based paints have an even more matt finish than "matt" paints, and are not so widely available. Silk is most often recommended as a base coat for decorative painting. Oil-based paint is best thinned with white spirit.

To find out how to get a base-coat colour, see Chapter Four, *Mixing Paints*. For the correct primer to use, see Chapter Three, *Preparing to Paint*.

## GLAZE

Transparent oil glaze is available premixed in tins from art and craft shops, as well as in some DIY centres and paint stores and by mail order. To this oil glaze, you add colour, usually in the form of oil-based paints, universal stainers or artist's oils. Artist's oils come in every hue imaginable, but are often costly due to the exotic pigments they employ. Liquid universal stainers, often used by professionals, are concentrated and thus often the least expensive option when colouring large quantities of glaze. They come in easy-to-control squeeze bottles. However, they come in less colours than artist's oils and, because they contain no drying agent, you shouldn't use more than 10 per cent.

The oil-based glazes in the recipes use eggshell paint or artist's oils to tint them. Eggshell paint helps prevent the finish from yellowing. When mixing up a glaze using eggshell, add around 2 or 3 parts of paint to around 7 parts glaze. You will then need to add 1 or 2 parts white spirit to get the correct consistency. With artist's oils you will need about a 9cm squeeze of paint to ½ litre oil glaze.

Dissolve the paint in a little white spirit before adding to glaze, then add white spirit to thin. But test before you start adding, and frequently as you add it in; too much will make the glaze run. See Chapter Four, *Mixing Paints*, for instructions.

Keep in mind that the proportions of paint to glazing liquid to solvent vary depending on the technique. For some, an especially watery and transparent glaze is desired; for others, a thicker consistency is essential. Glaze proportions may also differ from the proportions given in this book for a particular technique because of variations in the different brands of oil glaze. For best results, add solvent slowly, and reserve a little glazing liquid straight from the can, in case you overthin your mixture.

*Read the label on your oil glaze (and on all paint products).* Reading the label with the "Flagstone" recipe was crucial because the glaze was to be used on a floor, and the label indicated the oil glaze was suitable for that purpose. (Some oil glazes are, while others aren't.)

Glaze and paint labels also give you a host of important information: how much glaze or paint to buy for a project (usually in the form of how many square meters you can cover with one tin); how long paint or glaze takes to dry; and what kinds of safety precautions to take.

**Making your own glaze.** If you can't find ready-mixed oil glaze and you're at home "baking from scratch", you can make your own glaze with ingredients found in most art supply stores or mail-order art supply catalogues. The glaze, however, will dry slower and smell stronger.

To make the glaze, mix three parts turpentine to one part boiled linseed oil. (Linseed oil comes either boiled or raw; boiled is thicker and dries faster.) Then add a few drops of terebine dryer, and colour your glaze with paint or tints, as described above.

**Premixed coloured glazes.** Note that you can also sometimes get a limited selection of premixed coloured glazes. These, of course, will be much more expensive, and you won't have much control over colour. But they might be a good (i.e., quick and easy) way of "getting your feet wet" on practice boards or a small object.

**Salvaging old glaze.** When glaze gets old, a skin forms on top of it. Remove the skin by straining the glaze through cheesecloth or a disposable sieve.

**The leopard skin effect, achieved via flogging.**

GENERAL INFORMATION

## METALLIC PAINT

Don't ignore metallic finishes because you assume they will be expensive and take forever to get the hang of. As Chapter Six of this book shows, those fashionable new-yet-old metallic finishes you see in all the stores on picture frames and lots of other accessories are accessible and affordable. Imagine the glow they can add to a room or a piece of furniture—say, for instance, enlivening the wooden legs and trim on a sofa.

The traditional decorative painting technique of gilding does require costly materials such as gold leaf and takes special skill to apply. There are books that detail this advanced technique, but training and experience are crucial to good results.

Instead, you can get the look with gold paint. There are several types, none of which actually contain gold. One type combines bronze powder and lacquer-based medium. Applying the paint over an ochre-coloured base coat can help you achieve a truer "gold".

The simplest route to take is to buy metallic paint premixed; but you can also buy the powder and medium separately and mix your own. Note that the more powder you put in the mix, the more opaque the paint.

## VARNISH

Varnish is a final transparent layer that protects your decorative finish and makes it last longer. It also determines the sheen of your finish.

To varnish or not to varnish? Good question. Often, it's optional. Many finishes are sturdy enough without it, and many surfaces (ceilings, most walls) don't get enough traffic or handling to require it. From some finishes, such as bronze or copper verdigris, varnish would actually detract, its sheen (even a low-lustre one) looking out of place on a piece you've carefully "aged". And on a less-than-perfect wall that you've tried to camouflage with a flat, "textured" finish, varnish will give it a sheen that will underscore every defect.

On the other hand, as a shine-and-depth enhancer, it can only benefit certain finishes, no matter where you put them—marble, for example, as well as malachite, granite, and tile.

As a protector, it is indispensable for any faux-finished floor, tabletop, piece of furniture, cabinet, door, skirting, chair rail, or other hard-use area. Delicate découpage, whatever its location wouldn't be complete without several coats. And any finishes in "high-risk" areas, such

**The rain-streaked appearance of weathered metal like this can be replicated through the "aged-metal" techniques in Chapter Six.**

PAINTS AND TOOLS: THE BASICS

hallways or children's rooms, deserve a few coats just to insure that your artistic endeavours aren't wasted.

To prevent your painted finishes from cracking, apply varnish only to surfaces that have fully dried (see "Drying Times," page 33). The varnish coats in this book were applied with an extra-large paint pad. See page 95 for a photo and instructions on applying varnish this way.

You can also roll varnish on or paint it on with special varnishing brushes made to hold large quantities of varnish. Keep these brushes just for varnishing. They are hard to clean, and if you leave even a bit of paint in them, the next time you use them for varnishing, the old paint might come out. In addition, they hold too much paint for regular jobs.

Like paint, varnish is best applied in several thin coats. Sand lightly between coats with fine grade wet-and-dry abrasive paper. Also like paint, varnish comes with both oil and water base. There are many kinds, some of which are available in a range of finishes—matt, eggshell, silk, and gloss.

One drawback of varnish: it tends to yellow over time, especially in a room that gets little sunlight, and the more coats of varnish you apply, the more it can yellow. In addition, some of the varnishes that yellow the most are the ones that provide the greatest protection.

This is especially a problem if the colours of your finish are light and the finish is in a hard-use area. For some projects, you may have to strike a balance between appearance and protection. Especially if you are using white emulsion paint, or any oil-based paint colours that you will be applying a water-based varnish over, test the effect on samples to get an idea of the amount of yellowing. (It's a safer bet to leave your finish unprotected for a few weeks than to varnish with the wrong product.)

Some kinds of varnish, and even some brands within each kind, yellow much less than others and thus would be your best choice for delicately hued work. A list of varnish types often used for interiors is included here; it indicates the general degree of yellowing each type is known to produce. In general, water-based varnishes yellow less. Some brands of varnish say "non-yellowing" on the label, but this may not really be the case, especially over white paint.

**Which varnish to use will depend on your surface and your finish.**

GENERAL INFORMATION　31

Note, however, that varnish manufacturers are currently addressing the yellowing and durability quandary. Ask your paint dealer for further recommendations.

**Oil varnish.** This varnish can be used over oil- or water-based paints as long as the finish is completely dry. Thin oil varnish with white spirit. It dries to the touch in about three hours and dries completely in 12 to 24 hours. The higher the gloss, the more oil it contains and the slower it dries. Oil varnish, especially marine varnish, yellows. Avoid using it over light colours.

**Polyurethane.** This works well over all oil- and water-based paints with the exception of artist's oils. It is especially good over free-hand painting, such as the veining in marble, which might peel if left unprotected. Thin polyurethane with white spirit. Polyurethane yellows less than some varnishes, but it is not the best choice over pale shades. Wait at least 12 hours between coats.

**Acrylic Varnish.** Compatible only with water-based paints, it is acrylic medium (used for water-based glazes) thinned with water. It dries fast and is best rolled on so that it doesn't leave marks. It is odourless and yellows only slightly.

**Water Polyurethane.** Stronger than acrylic varnish, water polyurethane takes longer to dry. Thin it with water, if necessary. Yellowing is minimal.

**Polyurethane Gel Varnish.** Made for furniture, this is polyurethane in a gel state that you simply rub on over a completely dry finish with a cotton rag or foam pad, applying it in the direction of the wood grain.

**White Refined Beeswax.** Rub beeswax on the surface with a cotton or linen cloth. Let it set; then buff it with a clean cloth. This clear finish doesn't turn yellow. If it gets dirty, you can remove it without disturbing the paint below. It must, however, be reapplied often, as needed.

# How Much Paint?

Always buy or mix more than enough paint for base coats and glazes. Don't skimp here. Running out of paint in the middle of a wall will probably mean redoing the whole thing; the change in colour with a new batch may be noticeable, and a dark line will show where you left off. Besides, you'll need extra paint for touch-ups in the future. And you may want to include the same paint colours in other rooms at a later date to create a coordinated look for your home.

First determine the area of your project. Then, to estimate the amount of paint you will need for your two base coats, read the label on the paint can to see how many meters a tin covers. Generally, 2.5 litres of paint will cover about 32 meters when applied with a roller or brush. A litre of paint covers about 10 square meters. To be safe, however, subtract about 20 per cent from the estimate given on the tin.

For glaze, figure on about half the amount of paint you used for the base coat. (If a decorator applied the base coat, ask him or her how much paint was used.) The glaze is usually a single coat and requires a thinner application; so you should have some left over for repairs.

## Drying Times

Take drying times seriously—the success of your project will often depend on them. This is especially true for oil paint, but even emulsion paints don't dry immediately.

Keep in mind that there are two kinds of dry: dry to the touch and dry to the core, or cured. Paint dries from the top down; even if it feels dry on the surface, it might still be wet underneath. One layer must be cured before you add another. If a layer hasn't cured, and you recoat it, the second layer might bubble, peel, or crack. Or, especially when you are actively distressing a glaze, as in ragrolling, you might break through the base coat beneath, destroying your finish.

Estimating drying times is difficult because many factors come into play. Paint dries by oxidation: when combined with air and light, it is transformed from a liquid into a solid. So, the amount of light and the type of weather are important; paint won't dry as fast in the dark or in a humid atmosphere. The sheen of the paint also counts: matt paint dries more quickly than silk finish. How absorbent your surface is and how thickly you apply the paint also matter. If acrylic paint is thinned with water, it dries faster. If oil-based paint is coloured with artists's oils, it dries more slowly.

Here are some averages to give you an idea how much time to set aside for your projects. An oil-based undercoat dries to the touch in three to four hours, but is best left overnight before recoating—and even then it is not fully cured. An emulsion base coat, depending on its sheen, takes about 20 minutes to dry to the touch and about two hours to be fully cured.

To speed dry either oil- or water-based paint, use a fan in the room. For a sample or small surface, use a hair dryer.

To slow down the drying time of an oil-based coat or glaze, add a little linseed oil; but note that the more oil you add, the glossier the finish will be. To speed drying time, add terebine dryer, available from specialist paint stores—but don't make it more than 5 per cent of the total mix or the paint might crack.

With water-based glaze or paint, slowing drying time is a challenge. A good technique is to wet the walls with a sponge before you start painting. Working on a humid day or turning on a humidifier will make the glaze stay wet longer, as will blocking out direct sunlight. You can also add a bit more water to glaze or paint, but be careful that it doesn't run. And you might try adding an acrylic gel retarder, available in art supply stores, to water-based glaze; but be sure it constitutes less than 10 per cent of the total glaze solution or it will weaken the paint.

**The face mask at left filters out dust and particles. The face mask at right keeps out fumes.**

GENERAL INFORMATION         33

# TOOLS

A big part of the fun of decorative painting are all the tools you get to use. As in cooking, the more involved you get, the more paraphernalia you'll acquire.

A glance at the photo at the end of this chapter will give you an idea of the diversity of materials used to create the finishes in this book. Some of them you may already have, either in daily use or stowed in the garage, the remains of previous house-painting projects.

One option you'll see Nancy taking advantage of, particularly when working with oil-based paints, is the use of disposable tools such as foam brushes, roller covers, and paint trays. If you plan to do only a few decorative painting projects, or you don't have the time and commitment to the cleaning required when using quality painting tools, you may want to try this option. You may also want to take this route if you are sensitive to solvents because it will lessen the time you are exposed to them. (Environmentally speaking, it may be a dilemma; you don't need solvents for clean up, but you will create disposal problems.)

For convenience and cost-savings, you can also use everyday items instead of "official" painting paraphernalia. Paper plates can easily serve as painter's palettes. Plastic containers with lids can be reused as storage containers for paint and glaze.

To apply glaze in "additive" techniques or "distress" (remove) glaze for "subtractive" techniques, you'll use tools ranging from large feathers, a feather duster, and a paint scraper to sea sponges, paint brushes, and wide-ribbed corduroy. Once you're familiar with the basics of decorative painting, you may want to start checking around for items to use as tools to create your own unique finishes.

## Safety Measures

- Make sure your work area is well ventilated.

- When opening a tin of paint, wear goggles to prevent paint from splashing in your eyes.

- When sanding, or vacuuming up your work area after sanding, wear a mask designed to keep you from breathing in particles and dust. When working with oil- or alcohol-based products, using thinners, or spraying paint, especially if you are particularly sensitive to their vapours, wear a more elaborate face mask designed with a special filter to guard against fumes. The face masks come in different sizes; get the right size for you so that it gives a good seal. (See photo, page 33.)

- Wear rubber gloves to protect your hands against solvents. Surgical gloves are recommended. They usually come in small and large sizes; for dexterity, get the correct size for your hands.

- Keep a bucket of water and perhaps a fire extinguisher nearby when working with turpentine, shellac, and other flammable substances.

- Don't throw wet rags soaked in oil or solvents in the bin. Spread them out to dry outside or in a well-ventilated room.

For some techniques, specialized, sometimes-expensive paint brushes are traditionally used. Whenever possible, you'll find alternate suggestions of tools you can use instead right in the recipe.

Decorative painting tools also include items needed for preparation, paint mixing, and clean up. Preparation tools for painting a room include:

*Dust sheets or plastic sheeting to cover furniture and newspaper to protect floor; lightweight stepladder in good condition and scaffolding for large projects and ceilings; soft, absorbent all-cotton rags for cleaning; abrasive paper (in several grades) and a sanding block; tacky rag; vacuum cleaner or broom and dustpan; flexible filling knife and filler; steel ruler, metal straightedge, spirit level, chalkline, chalk pencil, or regular pencil, craft knife, and masking tape for measuring out designs; low-tack masking tape for covering areas you don't want to get paint on; paint roller, roller cover, and paint tray for priming and base-coating large surfaces.*

Note that the pile depth of the roller cover should be suited to the job: for example, short pile is generally for smooth surfaces. Medium pile usually works well on most surfaces, but check with your local paint store.

For paint and glaze mixing, you will need paint stirrers (old long-handled round brushes can work well or disposable chopsticks), plastic containers or paper bowls for mixing paint, and cardboard and white paper for trying out colours and techniques. For cleaning, have on hand extra all-cotton rags, water, white spirit or brush cleaner (depending on your paint type), plastic containers with lids for storing small amounts of leftover paints and glazes, and a spirit marker or stick-on labels to mark the contents of each container.

# Brushes

Many of the painting tools that you will be using will be brushes. As with all painting tools, you will find it easiest when you use the right type, size, and quality of brush for each job. In fact, in decorative painting, the brush can sometimes determine the success of a technique.

An example is the decorative painting technique called "stippling", in which you dab a brush over and over against a surface, covering the surface with fine dots. A large stippling brush, which looks something like a scrubbing brush, can be quite expensive. No other tool gives as soft and subtle an effect.

Other types of specialist brushes used for paint effects include fitches (similar to artists' oil-painting brushes), softeners (for subtle finishing of paint effects), draggers and floggers (long haired brushes used for creating texture) and grainers (for creating wood-grain effects).

Good quality decorating brushes are hand-crafted from natural pig bristle, the best being white hog bristle–known as "lily-bristle."

Gear the size of your brush to the job. To speed priming and base-coating of large, flat areas, you can use a roller.

If you use a brush, get the widest one possible (but not so wide that it overlaps the surface), and make sure you feel comfortable with it.

Brushes come in several shapes. For priming and base-coating large surfaces, use a straight-edged brush; for trim, a chisel-edged brush. To smooth a glaze that has just been applied, professionals often use a spatter or varnish brush.

Look for quality when choosing brushes. A good brush is thick and has bristles of various lengths, which allow it to hold more paint. The bristles should be springy, not stiff.

GENERAL INFORMATION

# The Wide Array of Tools Used in

PAINTS AND TOOLS: THE BASICS

# Decorative Painting

1. Paint tray
2. Paint tin for mixing and storing paints and glazes
3. Disposable bowls for holding paints and glazes
4. Paper plates to use as disposable paint palettes and to experiment on
5. Plastic container for mixing and storing paints
6. Paint roller
7. Paint roller covers
8. Paint stirrer
9. Plastic spoon—use back to rub masking tape guidelines firmly in place
10. Paint scraper and pads
11. Car-wash sponge
12. Spirit level for checking guidelines
13. Paint pads—available in various sizes
14. Metal graining combs
15. Sea sponges
16. Fume-filtering face masks with special filters
17. Plastic surgical gloves
18. Round brushes
19. Disposable foam brushes
20. Dust and particle filtering mask
21. Masking tape—available in many widths and degrees of tackiness
22. Electric tool for cutting stencils
23. Craft knife for cutting stencils
24. Stencilling spray adhesive to keep stencils in place while you work
25. Cheesecloth
26. Corduroy
27. Cotton rags
28. 1mm thick plastic dust sheet
29. Abrasive paper—available in many grades from coarse to fine
30. Household sponge
31. Brushes in several widths
32. Artist's brushes
33. Gold size over which to apply metallic foil
34. Silver foil
35. Chalk pencil and standard pencil for marking guidelines
36. Ready-mixed crackle glaze
37. Feather duster
38. Large feather

GENERAL INFORMATION

CHAPTER
THREE

PREPARING
TO
PAINT

Contrary to what you might think, the difference between a professional painted finish and an amateur attempt isn't always a matter of technique.

Where professional painters put their time and effort—for the biggest pay-off—is in surface preparation. In fact, they often budget more time for this than for the actual painting, just to get the perfect "canvas" for their work.

That's because they know from experience that in decorative painting each layer builds on the previous one to create that great final effect. Without care and neatness in your preparation, your surface can become a distraction, drawing attention to its imperfections rather than your handiwork. Worse still, poor preparation can even cause your finish to peel off or crack soon after you've completed it.

Allow enough time for preparation when you choose your project. How much time will depend on the size of your project and the condition of your surfaces. For instance, preparing an entire room, with surfaces in good condition, can take several days. Some tasks, like scraping and sanding, are painstaking; other tasks, like washing down walls, require drying time.

If your surfaces are in particularly poor condition, or if the job is especially large, you may want to do what many professional decorative painters do: hire an interior house painter to complete this crucial stage.

Your decision will, of course, be based on budget considerations, too. But keep in mind the time involved—yours might be more profitably spent on other things. It will also probably take an experienced professional, already familiar with tools and materials needed for various projects, less time.

Stripping wallpaper is a good example. Practise provides an edge here. What an experienced stripper can do in a few days might take a first-time do-it-yourselfer more than a week—after which you might not have much time, or as much enthusiasm, for your decorative painting.

If you decide to hire someone, you can use this chapter to help you decide what needs to be done, how long it will take, and the best way to communicate your needs to a painter. You can diagnose the condition of your surfaces, get an idea of effective treatments, then compare them to your painter's advice to be sure you get the quality of preparation your project demands. Take your painter's advice seriously. In preparation, practise counts more than theory. Each job is different, and sometimes past experience is the best guide.

Not all projects will require the same level of preparation. It depends on:
- the surface on which you'll paint (new or old, painted or unpainted, porous or nonporous)
- the paint you'll use (oil- or water-based)
- the painted finish you've selected (some, like ragging, hide imperfections much better than dragging, which needs a super-smooth surface)

What is preparation work? A multi-step process that can involve cleaning, filling, skim-coating, sanding, priming, and base-coating your surface. Depending on surface conditions and the finish you choose, you may skip or touch briefly on some steps. New walls, for instance, should require no cleaning except a light dusting and little or no filling.

Note that the order in which you perform some of the steps varies for different surfaces. For example, unpainted wood, brickwork, and plaster must be primed before sanding to seal them and keep them from getting scratched. But, before being primed, painted wood, brickwork, and plaster must first be filled and then sanded to roughen the old paint so that primer will adhere. See the chart at the end of this chapter for the order in which to perform the steps on various surfaces. Descriptions of each preparation step follow.

**In decorative painting, each layer builds on the previous one. Great-looking finishes result from exceptional attention to detail in the surface-preparation stage.**

GENERAL INFORMATION 41

# Stripping Furniture and Woodwork

**This kitchen gleams due to the fact that it was stripped down to the wood before it was painted.**

For painted furniture and woodwork in good condition, you can skip stripping and start sanding (see page 44). With old pieces and junk shop finds, however, this is not often the case. You will probably need to remove the varnish and paint before you can create a surface suitable for decorative painting. You then prime, fill, and sand the piece as you would for raw wood.

This is time-consuming work; so before you start, make sure the piece you plan to paint is structurally sound. Move it from side to side; lean on it; pay special attention to its legs and any moving parts, such as drawers or extension leaves. In many cases, you can repair a piece with problems; but if chances for a "full recovery" are doubtful, your best bet may be to find another object for your attention. Make sure the piece you choose will fit in the space in your home you've set aside for it (can it fit through the doorway, etc.).

There are several ways to strip wood. You can have it done professionally, perhaps by the dipping process in which pieces are placed in a tank of chemical stripper. You can do it yourself with a scraper and one of the many chemical strippers available at DIY and paint stores, or you can use a scraper and a heat gun.

Note that although a heat gun can save time, you must practice with it first to avoid scorching surfaces. Check home-repair guides for instructions and safety measures.

PREPARING TO PAINT

With chemical strippers, read the manufacturer's instructions very carefully before opening the tin. Many strippers contain strong solvents, so heed all safety precautions. Work in a well-ventilated area; wear goggles to protect your eyes from flying paint chips or splashing solvent; wear the kind of safety mask that guards against fumes as well as particles (see photo, page 36); and use chemical-grade rubber gloves to protect your hands (not surgical gloves—strippers will dissolve them).

Strippers soften paint and varnish so that they can be scraped off easily. Liquid gel stripper, which comes in tins, is particularly effective. Dip an old brush into the tin and paint a strip about 15cm long on your surface. Apply another 15cm strip and continue in this manner. Use the widest brush that will fit in the tin. Don't stroke back and forth—it reduces the effectiveness of the stripper.

See the manufacturer's instructions for the time the stripper takes to work after it is applied. Test a small patch to see if paint comes off easily. If it does, scrape it all off with a wide filling knife, wiping the knife after each pass. Stubborn finishes may require a second coat.

## Cleaning

This simple step is vital. It removes dirt from a surface so that paint can bond with it. Whether your surface is painted or unpainted, new or old, will determine how to clean it. For example, if you have new walls, just dust them, wipe them with a soft cloth, or use the soft brush attachment of a vacuum cleaner. For older painted walls and other surfaces in fairly good condition—a little peeling, a few small holes—it's a good idea to wash off any grease, smoke, or dust that has accumulated using sugar soap.

## Scraping

Don't remove paint from a surface unless it is absolutely necessary; the job is too difficult and time-consuming. But for old surfaces in poor condition you'll begin the cleaning process by scraping paint from them instead of washing them.

Hold a filling knife at a 45-degree angle, or a triangle scraper (see drawing, page 46) with the blade perpendicular to your surface, and drag it along. Apply firm pressure and keep scraping until you hit a spot where the paint holds well. Skip this area and move to the next. You can use the same technique—but pressing lightly instead of firmly—to smooth new plaster walls.

## Stripping Wallpaper

Even if the quality of the walls underneath is particularly poor, you are probably best off removing wallpaper rather than painting over it. The reason: the wallpaper could eventually peel off and ruin your finish.

To remove wallpaper, first test to see if it can be removed dry, which is sometimes possible. In most cases, however, you start by soaking the walls thoroughly with a large brush and hot water. This may take several applications. You can add a commercial wallpaper-stripping compound to the water for extra power. Then, with a filling knife, begin stripping the paper off, working across rather than down the wall.

To remove several layers of paper, it is best if you hire a steam stripper. This machine boils water and produces steam that softens wallpaper paste quickly. Starting at the bottom of the wall, soften one strip at a time and then scrape it off with a wide scraper.

# Sanding

Sanding evens surfaces so that they are smooth to the touch. It also helps paint bond with a surface. There are many grades of abrasive paper, for a wide range of jobs—00 grade paper for sanding floors, 600 grade for smoothing varnish, and up to 1200 grade for fine work. Check with your local paint or hardware store for the grade your surface requires.

To sand evenly, use a sanding block (see drawing). You can buy one, usually a wood or cork block. Sometimes it comes with a long pole, which makes big jobs less tiring. You can also make a sanding block by taping abrasive paper to a piece of scrap wood or a child's building block.

Electric sanders are available, but be sure to use them carefully. They tend to move fast and can quickly make a surface uneven if handled improperly. Practise first. Beginners will find them easiest to use on small horizontal surfaces, such as dresser- or tabletops.

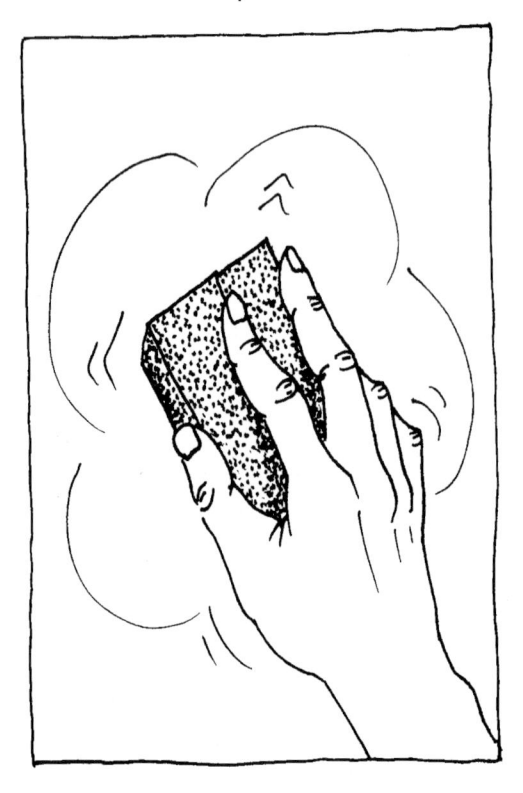

# Priming

Primer seals surfaces from dirt, fungus, and humidity. It saturates them with paint so that they can take on colours. And it makes them nonporous so that you'll need fewer coats of paint to get the colour you want.

There is a primer for almost every surface, from laminate to glass to brick. Some primers are fire retardant. Others, designed for exterior work, help combat the effects of adverse weather. There are metal primers that prevent rust and help paint adhere to slick surfaces. (See the chart at the end of this chapter for recommended primers for various surfaces.) If you want to apply decorative paint to an unusual surface, ask your DIY store or paint shop which primer to use.

Primer comes in three types: water, oil, or (less commonly) alcohol-based. This makes priming a good stage at which to decide on a paint system—water or oil—to work with. (See Chapter Two, *Paints and Tools*, for a review of each system.) Your choice depends very much on the decorative-painting technique you select and the surface you'll be painting on. Furniture, for instance, is done in oils because of their greater durability. If you know which finish you're going to use right now, turn to the recipe for it in Part Two of this book, and see whether its chart recommends water- or oil-based paints.

If you haven't picked a recipe yet, but must continue preparatory work, remember this: *you can apply oil- or water-based paints over water- or alcohol-based primers, but only oil paints over oil primer.* In addition, most of the recipes in this book call for a water-based undercoat of emulsion. So, play it safe, and start with either a water- or an alcohol-based primer. But first, of course, be sure your surface is compatible with these types. Consult the chart at the end of this chapter or check with your local paint store.

Primer is usually white, which is fine in most cases. In general, the lighter your undercoats, the nicer your finish.

Pale undercoats bring more light into a colour and make it richer, while dark undercoats can dull it. Renaissance masters knew this well; they used light washes of colour to make their paintings glow.

But if you plan a dark base-coat, you may want to darken your primer to make coverage easier. You can have it tinted at a paint store. For instance, red paints don't always cover well; by having your primer tinted light pink, you're closer to the colour you desire for a basecoat and may even need one less coat to achieve it. You can also tint primer yourself with artist's oils or acrylics, depending on the type of primer—oils for oil, acrylics for water-based.

Most primers come in both interior and exterior grade. In almost all cases, you'll want interior grade. (Refer to the chart at the end of this chapter to see if your surface is an exception.)

One primer—shellac—comes only in interior grade. It is alcohol-based and available in several colours including white, which dries transparent; and button polish, which has an orange tint. Knotting, for scaling knots in wood before priming, is also made from shellac.

Shellac is one of the best primers for decorative painting because it dries to the touch in about 15 minutes and can be recoated in about a half-hour. Check the label of the product you buy for precise drying times. Because it dries so fast, however, you may have difficulty smoothing out brush or roller marks. Also, it can't easily be sanded down. So put it on with a fine roller and do not go back over it. Disposable rollers are particularly recommended with shellac because it is hard to clean. If you must clean tools or wipe up spills, use methylated spirit. Wear a mask that protects against toxic vapours (not just particles, see page 34) when working with shellac.

Shellac is particularly good for sealing plaster. It dries quickly, cutting down on lost time between coats. If, for instance, you used an oil-based primer, you'd have to wait up to 12 hours between coats and apply three or four coats because the plaster absorbs so much primer. But with shellac, you'd need only two coats.

A word about metal primers: there are rusting and nonrusting metals, and each has its own primer. For example, iron, which rusts, either comes factory primed or needs a rust-proofing primer-sealer, which is usually grey or orange.

In addition to preventing rust, it dries fast and provides a surface to which paint can easily adhere. Aluminum, on the other hand, doesn't rust, but it does need a primer that helps paint bind to its surface. Both primers emit extremely toxic fumes, so wear a face mask designed to protect against them while you work.

**Surface preparation is most important in the water closet, where surfaces face daily exposure to dampness and humidity.**

GENERAL INFORMATION

# Filling

Many surfaces need filling. The process involves filling holes, cracks, and nicks with a fine-grade filler, plaster, or a mix of the two. There are many ready-mixed fillers on the market today made to different formulations. They come in tins, tubes, or tubs. For best results ask your paint store what professional painters use.

When filling a crack in an old wall, you must fill it properly so that it won't soon reappear in your freshly painted surface. First, insert a triangular scraper into one end of the crack; then, run the scraper along the crack, enlarging it evenly to about 3mm deep. Wipe the crack with a damp sponge. Apply the filler compound in two or three coats, letting it dry between applications so that the filler will hold better.

Because the filler shrinks as it dries, overfill the crack. If the filler forms a bump, you can sand it smooth after it dries, then dust the surface with a soft brush. Apply primer over any areas you have filled. (Shellac primer is recommended for this because it dries fast.) The primer will prevent filled holes and cracks from appearing as dull spots in your painted finish.

After you've filled and sanded, dust the surfaces and vacuum the floor so that dust doesn't get into your paint. You can also sprinkle water on the floor to trap the dust, then sweep it up with a broom. To dust walls thoroughly, painters often use a hand broom.

For furniture, they use a "tacky rag", a slightly sticky cloth available in hardware and paint stores. (It is best to use it gently because it can leave a film on surfaces.) An alternative to a tacky rag is a plain, clean cotton cloth dampened with water.

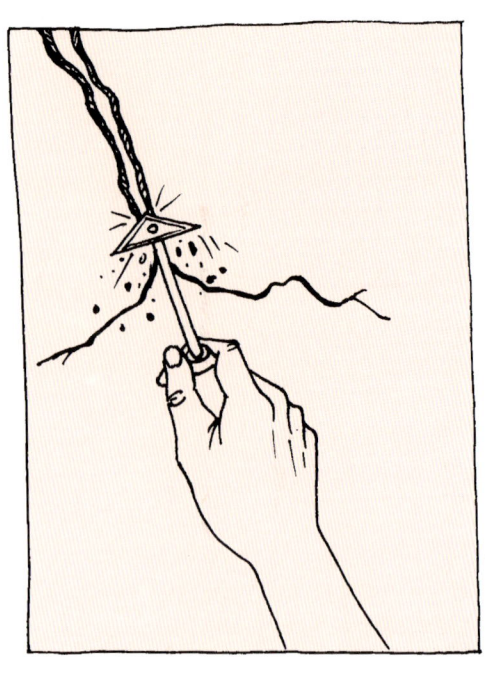

**1.** To fill a crack, first enlarge it evenly with a triangular scraper to about 3mm. Cut a dovetail-shaped groove so that filler will fill it securely.

**2.** Before applying filler, wipe the crack with a damp sponge or mist with spray bottle. Scoop the filler from the container onto large filling knife, scrape a bit of filler at a time onto a smaller knife, and fill the crack.

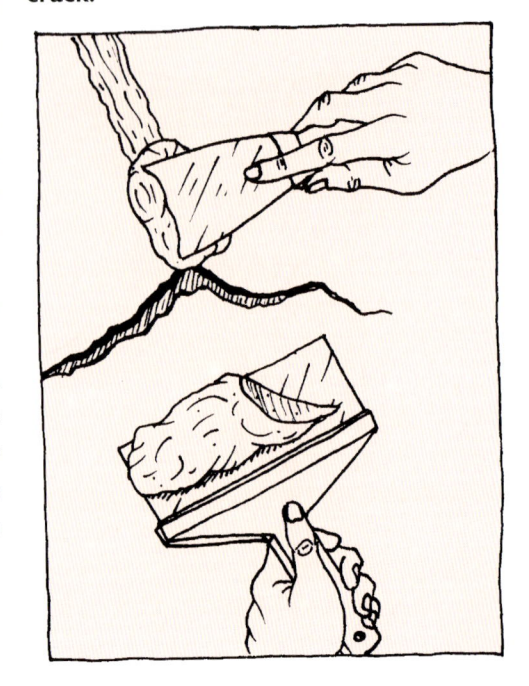

**PREPARING TO PAINT**

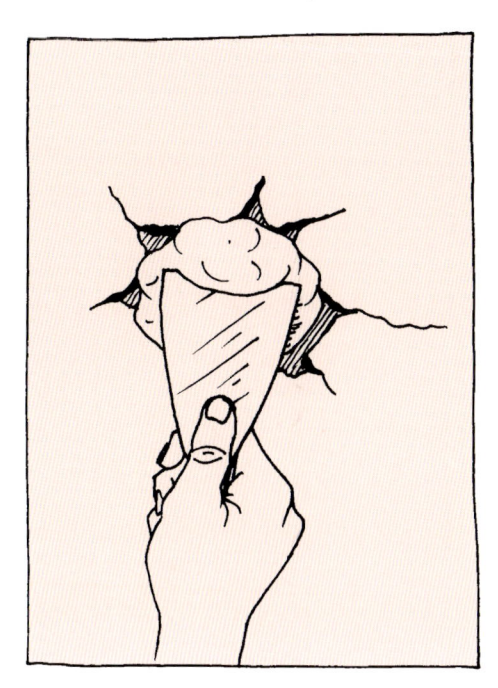

**3. For a round crack, push filler into centre to fill it.**

**4. Next, work the filler out to edges. Let it dry, then sand it flush with surface.**

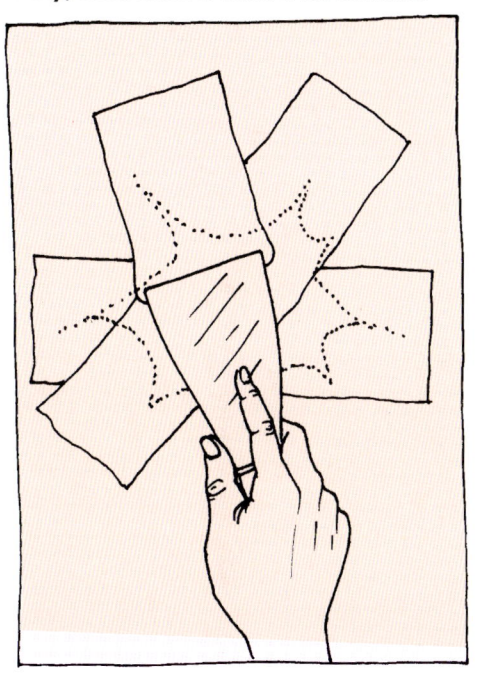

# Skim-Coating

After your surfaces are filled and primed, step back and examine them. Now that they're all one colour, you can see what you have to work with. Keep in mind that their condition will strongly influence how your decorative finish will look. Hold a light up to a surface, and its imperfections will become apparent.

For some finishes, especially a gloss like moiré or realistic marbling, your surface may still not be smooth enough. In that case you can skim-coat it. This process is difficult and time-consuming—and thus best done by a professional—but it will give you a very smooth surface.

Skim-coating is done over the primer (see drawings, page 48). Because it is a thin coat of filler, you probably won't have to reprime afterward unless you've applied several skim coats to obtain a smooth surface. This isn't advisable, however. The more skim coats you apply, the weaker your surface becomes and the more likely it is to crack.

You skim-coat with filling compound. Hold a large filling knife flat and run it lightly over the walls, filling in any gaps and dents with filler. Working in 90cm sections, apply the compound in a long sweep. Then clean off the knife and drag the clean blade back over the surface; the filling will remain.

Skim-coating is frequently used for flat surfaces like walls, tabletops, and wood furniture. Say you strip, prime, and sand a piece to prepare it for marbling, but its wood grain shows through too strongly. You can skim-coat it following the length of its grain and dragging the knife over the surface at a slight angle so that you fill only the grain. Sand again, and apply a second skim coat, if needed.

GENERAL INFORMATION

## TAPING A CRACK

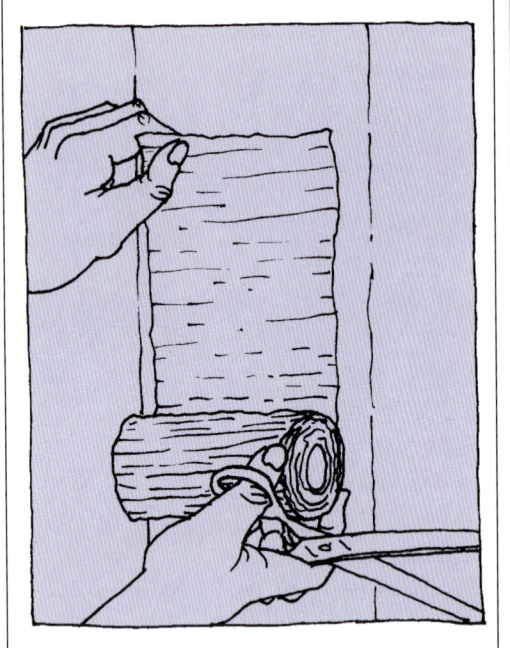

1. Even a carefully filled crack can reappear over time. For extra protection, tape the crack after filling it. Once the filled crack is dry, cover a thin coat of filler with gauze, and flatten it to set it.

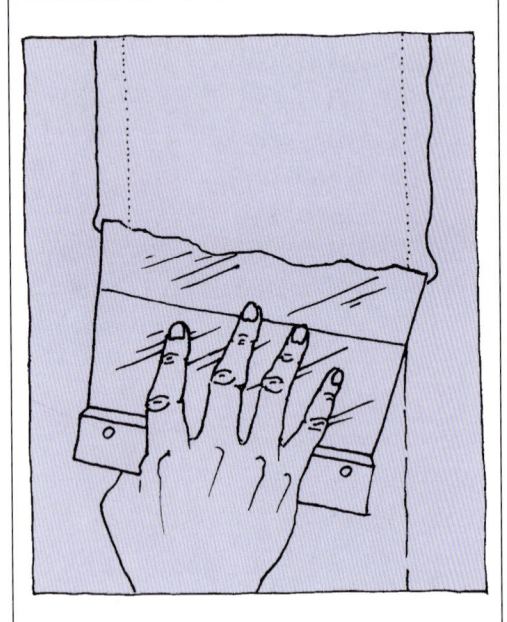

2. After sanding smooth, skim-coat (*skim-coating means applying a thin coat of plaster*) with a wide filler knife over the gauze to cover it.

## SKIM-COATING A WALL

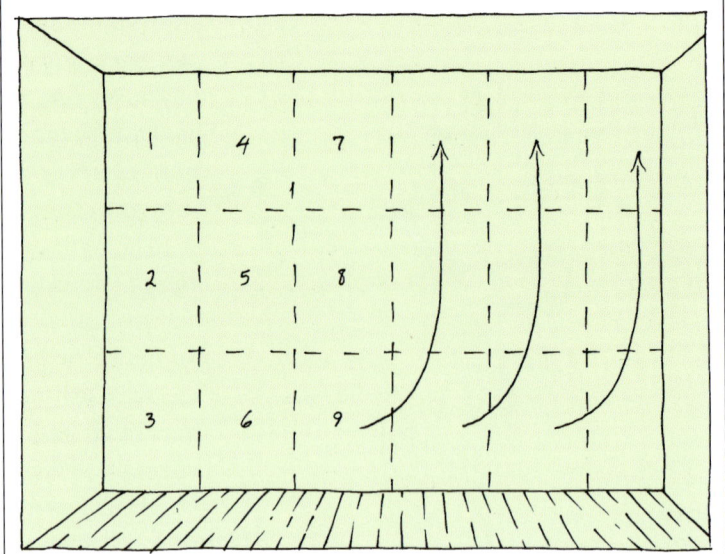

This diagram illustrates how to skim-coat a wall. Work in sections about 60-90cm, starting in the top left-hand corner if you are right-handed or the top right-hand corner if you are left-handed. Move down the wall in vertical rows.

## PAINTING A ROOM

When painting a room, follow the order professionals use: start with the ceiling, then do the walls, window frame, doors and door frame, cornice mouldings, fireplace, skirting, and floor. When doing a floor, work out toward the door so that you don't paint yourself into a corner.

**PREPARING TO PAINT**

# Base-Coating

At this point, select from Part Two the recipe you will execute. Read the chart for that recipe to see if your base coat should be oil or emulsion. (In most cases, it will be emulsion.)

Also decide on your base-coat and glaze colours now. If you'd like to reproduce a painted finish in the same colours used in its recipe, bring this book to your local paint store and show the paint mixer the colour swatches you desire. The paint mixer will be able to create a colour very similar to the one you have chosen.

If you prefer another colour combination, first look at paint charts. With the wide range of colours available today, you may well be able to find the base-coat colour you want ready-mixed. If not, you can buy a small amount of the colour closest to what you'd like and lighten, darken, or otherwise alter it with artists' oils or universal stainers, which come in many colours and can be used with oil- and water-based paints. When you get the colour you want, paint a sample on a board, take it to the paint store, get it colour-matched, and have larger quantities mixed.

Before you do, pick and mix samples of your glaze colours. Paint sample boards with your base-coat and glaze colours using the technique you've chosen. Study them in various lights to see if you get the colour you want. For more on mixing paints, see Chapter Four. (A detailed guide to mixing base coats and glazes is available in the first edition of *Recipes for Surfaces*, page 73.)

After adjusting the colours as needed, you are ready to apply your base coat. In all cases, you should apply at least two coats of paint.

For surfaces larger than a set of double doors, apply base coats with a roller. Apply base coats in criss-cross fashion, especially on flat surfaces like panelling, doors, and tables. Paint down first, then across, then down again with a brush that is almost free of paint. (Note: don't paint top and bottom edges of wood doors. This lets wood breathe and prevents warping—plus ensuring that the door still opens!)

Criss-crossing is simple with a brush, but not as easy with a roller. With water-based paints—which, because they dry faster, tend to leave brush or roller marks—work in 1.2m sections and go over the second layer in the same direction with a dry roller while the paint is still wet.

Before starting a large project that requires many litres of paint, pour the paint from all the 2.5 litre paint tins into a 15 litre bucket (available at paint and hardware stores) or a plastic rubbish bin. Mix thoroughly, then pour paint back into the 2.5 litre tins until needed. This extra effort helps ensure satisfying results. Despite colour differences among paint batches, you'll get exactly the same hue throughout your project.

Paint taken directly from the tin is too thick to work with. Although it covers well, it also drips, leaves marks, and dries slowly. For a smoother finish and shorter drying time between coats, thin your first coat 10 to 15 per cent with the appropriate solvent (water for emulsion, white spirit for oil). Add solvent a bit at a time so that paint doesn't get too thin. (If it does, leave it out uncovered until the solvent evaporates.) Stir the paint well, and test its consistency with a brush.

Thin your second coat so that it is almost as thin as your first—but never thinner, or the paint will crack when it dries. Wait until the first coat is completely dry. Give yourself plenty of time in which to finish your project. Whenever possible, let each coat dry before applying the next one.

**GENERAL INFORMATION**

# Applying a Base Coat: Step-by-Step

1. Before using roller to apply base coat to primed wall, paint edge of wall next to moulding with a 5cm household paint brush. Rolling paint evenly to moldings is impossible; "cutting" a line provides straight edge from which to work.

2. Always work from top of wall down, to avoid dripping paint on freshly coated surface. Once edges are trimmed, you can fill in rest of wall using roller.

3. To base-coat door, start with panels. Dip your brush into paint, coating it well. Discharge brush by painting three vertical strokes on top panel. Next, without re-dipping brush, work first from left to right, then top to bottom, and left to right again in criss-cross fashion to smooth paint and prevent colour variations. Do lower door panel in same manner; then paint horizontal members, then vertical members, and finally door frame.

4. With a slanted 5cm brush, tackle the chair rail. As with any surface, paint mouldings from top down to prevent drips on just-coated areas. After chair rail do the skirting.

5. Do floor last. Sand surface smooth.

6. Before you begin painting floor, mask skirting once it has dried to keep floor paint from getting on it.

PREPARING TO PAINT

GENERAL INFORMATION

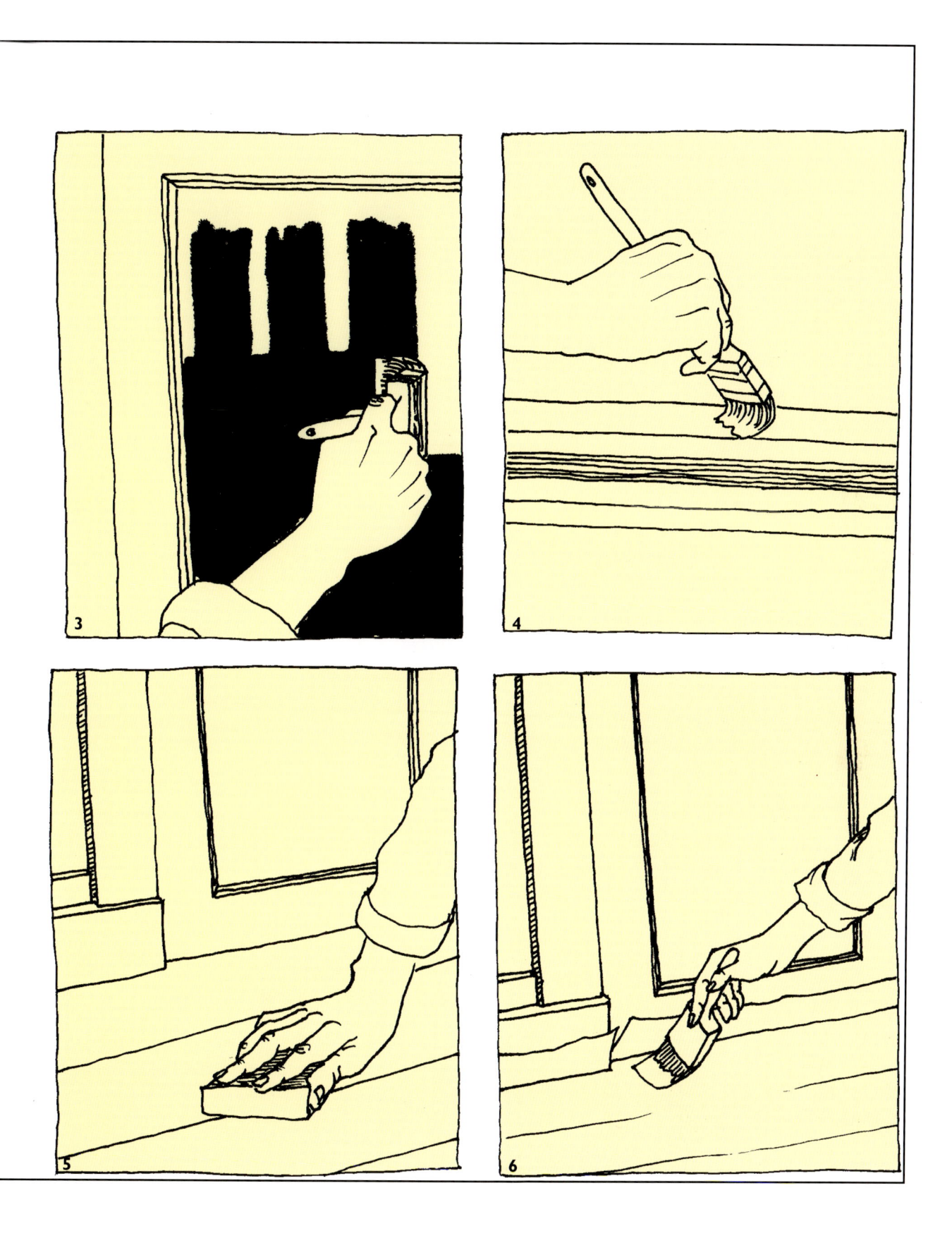

# Dividing a Wall into Panels

On many of the recipes, you'll see that a finish is recommended not just for walls, but for wall panels. Marbling, for example, is especially effective presented that way. The two illustrations show one of many ways you can divide a fireplace wall into panels. Keep in mind that a variation of this pattern might better suit your particular wall.

**Draw your design to scale on graph paper first. Start drawing from the centre of the wall and work out. Then transfer your design to the wall using a chalkline to "snap" on first the vertical lines and then the horizontals. (See next page for how to use a chalkline.)**

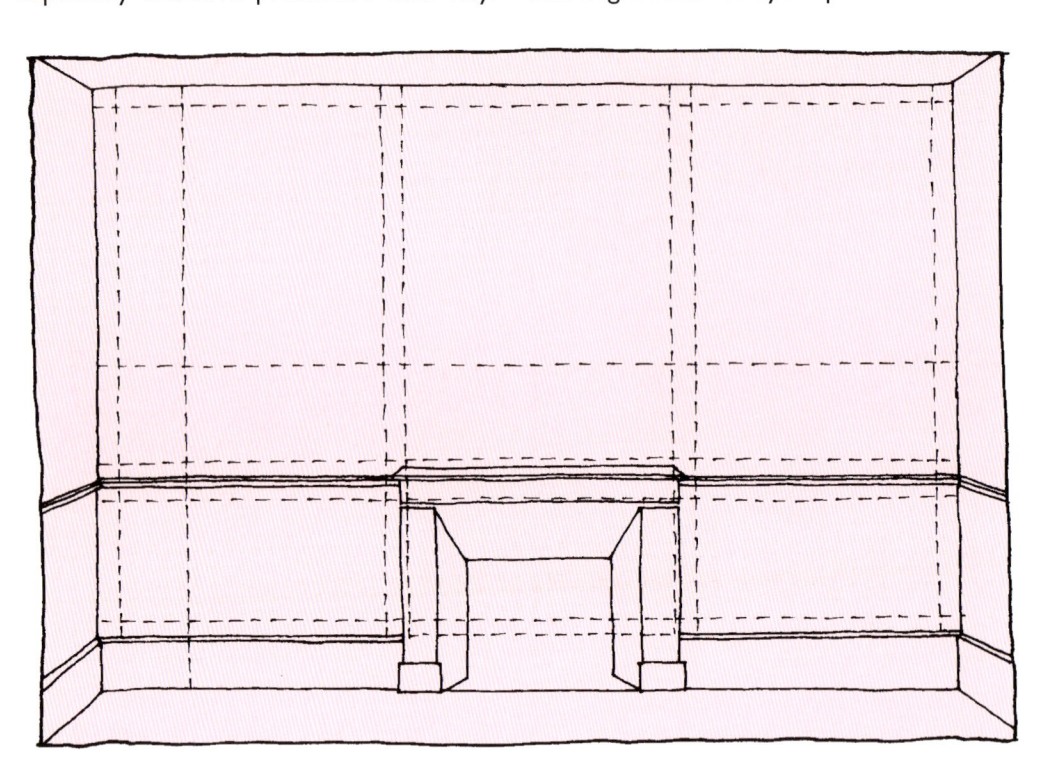

**Here is the finished drawing transferred to the wall. Walls divided into panels are often wood-grained, usually in more than one type of wood for an inlaid look. Try "figured" graining (done with a graining tool) for the panels and straight graining (done with a graining comb) for the frame.**

PREPARING TO PAINT

## Painting a Chair

Note that one of the recipes in this book ("Crackle Glaze", page 157) is demonstrated on a chair. In general, painting furniture will take longer than any other project. That's because of all the curves and angles—and surface imperfections are both easier to create and more noticeable on these smaller surfaces. And since most furniture is painted in oil-based paint and varnished for durability, imperfections tend to stand out due to the high sheen the paints give the surface.

Applying paint to a chair can be tricky for novice painters, since most of us have gained our painting experience on large, flat expanses, like walls. The key is to paint one element at a time—each leg of the chair, each side rail, seat, etc.—without getting paint on any other part. If paint does lap over from one element to the next, you must wipe it off immediately. That extra paint would cause an uneven surface if you let it dry and painted over it.

To help keep you neat, paint elements first from one edge toward the centre, then from the other edge in, blending paint in the middle. Use a small flat brush scaled to the size of your project for main areas and a soft, pointed sable brush on carved areas, if needed.

## Loading and Holding Brushes and Rollers

**BRUSHES** Pour paint from the large storage container into a small bucket or paint kettle. This lets you keep most of your paint covered so that it doesn't dry or form a skin on top. In addition, if debris falls into your open paint bucket, the rest of the batch will not be contaminated. Dip your brush into the bucket so that about two-thirds of the bristles are covered with paint. Then wipe the brush on the inside edge of your bucket to prevent drips. For priming and base-coating, hold your brush at a slight angle and apply moderate, even pressure.

Grasp the brush low on the handle near the bristles for a firm grip. Avoid using excessive pressure, even in corners and other hard-to-reach places.

**ROLLERS** Fill a roller tray so that no more than half its ribbed bottom is covered with paint. Dip the roller into the paint at the shallow end of the tray and work it back and forth a few times above the paint line to remove excess paint and prevent drips. Place the roller against the wall, and roll it over the surface in long, even strokes.

### HOW TO USE A CHALKLINE

Chalklines let you mark easily erased straight lines on large surfaces. You can buy chalklines at DIY stores, hardware stores, and paint shops. They are small boxes containing 1500-3000cm of string on a reel. Some of them need to be filled with chalk or talcum powder; others however, come filled with blue chalk that is difficult to wipe off. If you get one of these, empty it out and refill the box with a mix of three-fourths talcum powder and one-fourth blue chalk. The line produced will be more visible on light surfaces yet easy to remove with a damp cloth.

You'll need a partner—one to hold the box, the other to hold the end of the string. Stretch the string along the surface to be marked, pulling the string tight so it is taut and flat against the surface. Then one person should snap the string hard by pulling it 60-90cm off the surface and letting it go so that when the string hits the surface, it leaves a powdery line.

# How to Prepare Surfaces

| MATERIAL | CLEANING | PRIMING, SANDING, FILLING, SKIM-COATING | BASE COAT |
|---|---|---|---|
| Raw wood (old furniture, stripped; new furniture and mouldings, unpainted; doors, panelling, cabinetry) | 1. Dust lightly with hand broom or soft-brush attachment on vacuum cleaner.<br>2. Remove any oil from the surface of oily hardwoods such as teak with white spirit immediately before priming. | 1. Seal knots in wood with shellac or "knotting".<br>2. Prime surface to harden pores and seal wood. If you don't know wood species, or if it is tropical wood, use aluminum wood primer or shellac. For other wood, oil-based primer recommended.<br>3. Sand primer, dust surfaces, sweep area.<br>4. Fill and skim-coat, if needed, with filler.<br>5. Sand surface lightly, dust surface, sweep area. | Oil-based paint recommended for wood. Emulsion can be used only over shellac or acrylic primer.<br>Note: on small surfaces such as furniture, apply with brush instead of roller. |
| Painted wood (furniture, doors, panelling, moulding, etc.) | 1. Wash with sugar soap to remove dirt and grease.<br>2. Let dry about a day. Note: test sugar soap on small area first to see how it affects painted surface.<br>3. Scrape, if needed.<br>4. Rub down with fine wet-and-dry paper to provide a key.<br>5. Rinse with clean water and allow surface to dry thoroughly. | 1. Fill areas of painted surface in poor condition.<br>2. Skim-coat, if necessary.<br>3. Touch up filled and skim-coated areas with primer to seal them. Prime any areas where raw wood has been exposed. (You need not prime over painted wood in good condition.)<br>Note: kind of primer to use depends on paint already on surface. If water-based, use oil or water-based primer. If oil, use oil primer. If you're not sure, use oil. | Use oil- or emulsion-based, depending on primer you used and technique you've chosen. |
| Unpainted brickwork (walls) | 1. Dust lightly with hard broom or soft-brush attachment on vacuum cleaner. | 1. Fill and skim-coat, if you want very smooth finish. (If you apply more than two skim coats, reprime.)<br>2. Prime: shellac recommended, but oil-based or emulsion primer can be used. | Oil or emulsion, depending on primer used and technique chosen.<br>Note: oil-based coat can be applied over all three primers, but use emulsion base coat only over water-based primer. |

PREPARING TO PAINT

# How to Prepare Surfaces

| MATERIAL | CLEANING | PRIMING, SANDING, FILLING, SKIM-COATING | BASE COAT |
|---|---|---|---|
| Painted brick-work (walls) | 1. Wash with sugar soap if very dirty.<br>2. Leave to dry for about a day.<br>Note: test on small area first to see how sugar soap affects painted surface. | 1. If needed, fill holes and cracks. Touch up filled areas with primer.<br>2. Skim-coat if you want very smooth finish; then prime.<br>3. Depending on condition of painted surface, and if you'll paint light colour over dark one, you may want to seal whole area with coat of primer. (See "Painted wood, *Priming*", page 54, for kind to use.) | Oil- or emulsion-based, depending on primer used and technique chosen. |
| Unpainted plaster (new walls, architectural details, ornaments, sconces, pedestals, capitals, etc.) | 1. Dust new plaster lightly with soft-bristle brush. Dust old plaster with hard-bristle brush.<br>2. Sand flat surfaces lightly, only if needed, taking care not to scratch surface.<br>3. Dust with soft-bristle brush. | 1. Fill if necessary.<br>2. Prime with few coats of multi-purpose primer or white shellac. For shellac, use disposable roller or brush, depending on surface size.<br>Note: for small carved surfaces, apply several coats of oil-based primer, thinned. | Oil-based recommended to seal surfaces from humidity, but emulsion can be used. |
| Painted plaster (old walls, architectural details, ornaments, sconces, pedestals, capitals, etc.) | 1. Wash with sugar soap. Avoid areas of exposed raw plaster.<br>2. Leave to dry for at least two days, especially if paint is chipped and water has seeped into plaster. | 1. Fill holes and cracks. Touch up areas with primer.<br>2. Skim-coat if you want very smooth surface; then prime.<br>3. Depending on surface condition, and if you're painting light colour over dark one, you may want to seal whole area with coat of primer.<br>Note: kind of primer to use depends on paint already on surface. If emulsion, use oil or emulsion primer. If oil, use oil primer. If you're not sure, use oil. | Oil-based recommended to seal surfaces from humidity. |

GENERAL INFORMATION

# How to Prepare Surfaces

| MATERIAL | CLEANING | PRIMING, SANDING, FILLING, SKIM-COATING | BASE COAT |
| --- | --- | --- | --- |
| Laminates, plastics, and resins (kitchen cabinets and counters, appliances, tabletops, pedestals, capitals, light fixtures, etc.) | 1. Wipe down with methylated spirits.<br>2. Wash with sugar soap, rinse well, let dry. | 1. Roughen surface by sanding with 150-grade abrasive paper.<br>2. Apply "surface duller" such as acetone. (Wear gloves, goggles, and face mask, and take safety precautions with these flammable solvents.)<br>3. Prime with plastic-grade primer. | Oil-based recommended for durability and compatibility with oil-based primer. |
| Closely woven canvas | None. | 1. For large floorcloth, you can stretch canvas by stapling it to wall, but you will need scaffolding to work on it. Place inexpensive fabric and plastic sheet behind canvas to cushion it and create smooth surface for sanding.<br>2. Sand canvas lightly.<br>3. Prime canvas with synthetic gesso, available in art supply shops, or with standard emulsion primer. Apply two coats. Thin first coat about 30 per cent and second coat about 10 per cent. | Two base coats of emulsion paint. |
| Other fabrics (T-shirts, curtains, etc.) | 1. Wash, iron, and press, if necessary. | None. | Textile paint, using special brushes with stiff, short hair, available in art supply shops. |
| Paper (cardboard for samples—hot-press with silk-finish recommended) | 1. Dust lightly, if needed. | 1. Oil-based primer. (Do not use water-based primer.)<br>2. Sand lightly. | Two coats of oil- or emulsion paint, whichever is used for your technique. Note: in making samples, you can put water-based paints over oil—paper will absorb most of oil and results don't need to be durable. |

# How to Prepare Surfaces

| MATERIAL | CLEANING | PRIMING, SANDING, FILLING, SKIM-COATING | BASE COAT |
|---|---|---|---|
| Papier-mâché, papers for making your own wallpaper, gift wrap, etc. | 1. Dust lightly, if needed. | 1. Prime with oil-based primer. | Oil-based paints. |
| Metal, rusting — iron (furniture, accessories, stair rails) | 1. Go over entire surface with wire brush to remove rust, if necessary.<br>2. Wash new, factory-primed surfaces with sugar soap. | 1. Use rust-proofing metal primer. | Oil-based paints. Check manufacturer's labels to see which paints are compatible with primer. |
| Ceramic (baths, lavatories, tiles, old appliances, etc.) | 1. Remove protective grease finish from new and unprimed surfaces with acetone. Note: acetone is flammable and toxic. Take safety precautions: wear face mask, goggles, and gloves. | 1. Use primer for non-rusting metals to help paint adhere to surface. | Oil-based. Ceramic spray paint is recommended. Make a sample on tile to test paint for adherence and durability. |
| Metal, non-rusting—aluminum (appliances, cabinets, etc.) | 1. Wash with sugar soap. | 1. To roughen surface, sand with heavy-grade paper in circular motion. | Oil-based. Spray paint will give a good finish. |
| Glass (tabletops) | 1. Clean with spray window cleaner to dissolve grease.<br>2. For tough jobs, use cream or powdered cleanser. Rinse well. | None. | Use sign painter's lettering enamel. Paint on underside of glass. Caution: test paint on glass for durability. Finish can scratch off. Glass is nonporous and, thus, less durable than, say, wood or brickwork. |

GENERAL INFORMATION

CHAPTER FOUR

# MIXING PAINTS

Over the past few years the increasing popularity of decorative painting has turned it from an art practised by professionals into a craft do-it-yourselfers have heartily embraced.

One area where this change is most apparent is in mixing paints. Today, there are many more ready-made products on the market that make the decorative-painting experience easier. And the options are still evolving. Spurred by environmental concerns with oil paints and the less-than-earth-friendly solvents they require, companies are developing new water-based products with the best properties of oils while still being safe to use and easy to clean up.

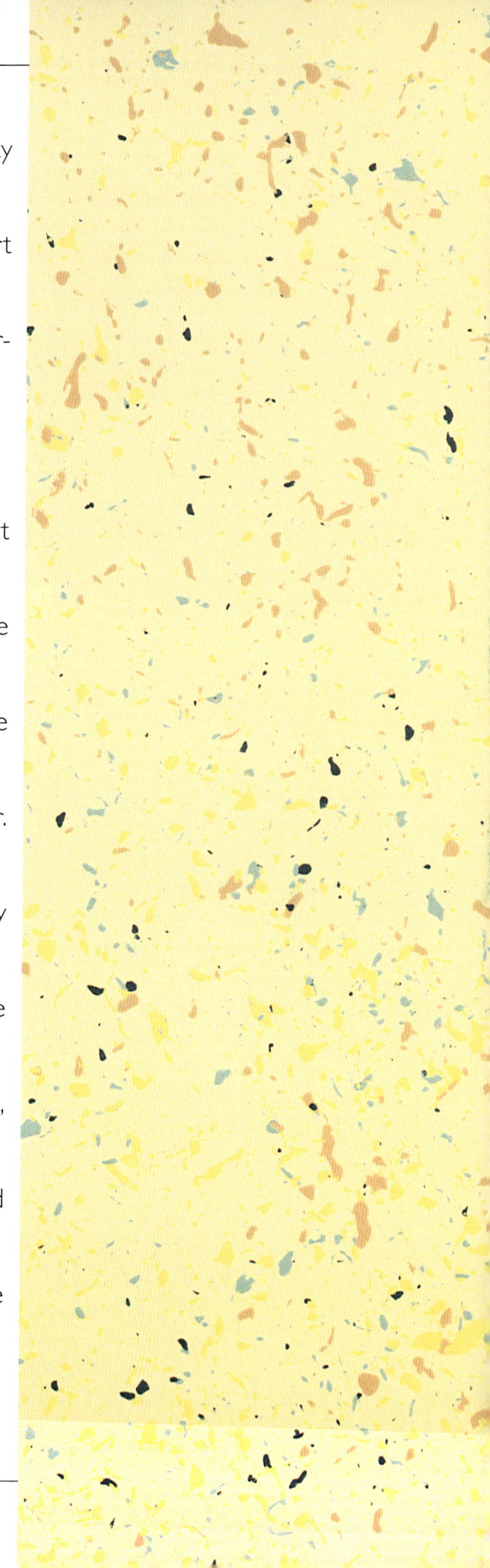

All this leaves you with some decisions to make. The biggest choice is the same one you face in the kitchen. Are you the buy-a-box-of-cake-mix type, or do you believe in doing everything from scratch?

There's no need for guilt here. There are simply two different approaches. You can go to a paint shop, pick up the paints you need, and get started on your project. Or, if you want the full experience of decorative painting, you can mix your paints yourself.

As in cooking, both approaches may be right for you at different times. Base your decision on the amount of time you have, your budget, your skill level, and your goals.

For example, if you want to decorate in a hurry, go the ready-made route. However, if you want to devise a unique colour scheme for your home based on a prized Oriental rug or beloved heirloom, you'll benefit from the full colour-mixing experience.

Before you start mixing paints, read Chapter One, *Colour*. You can also refer to the first edition of *Recipes for Surfaces* for a detailed guide to what supplies you'll need to get started and how to go about it.

There is, of course, a middle ground. You might want to try customizing your paints by tinting them slightly. To alter a emulsion base coat or water-based glaze, you can use artist's acrylics or universal stainers (but make stainers less than 10 per cent of your total paint mix or paint won't dry properly).

For an oil-based undercoat or oil glaze, you can use artist's oils, or universal tints (less than 10 per cent of total mix). You may still, however, prefer to go to your local paint store and have colour adjustments made up (especially for large quantities).

# Base Coats

There are several ways to get the base coat colour you want. The simplest involves going to the paint store and having the paints mixed for you.

Colours for the finishes in this book have been selected with many of today's most popular decorating styles in mind. So, in some instances, you may want to reproduce a finish just as it appears. All you have to do then is take this book with you to a paint shop or DIY store and show them the diamond-shaped "paint chip" found under the "Base Coat" section on the recipe card; a similar colour can be mixed for you. We have given suggestions for paint colours for each paint effect in the paint swatches that are located next to the colour names. Ordinary printing does not allow us to show absoluteley accurate colour swatches, but by using these as reference you can get very close to the colour scheme used for effects in this book. You should be able to get a close match from many different paint manufacturers. By bringing the swatches to a paint shop, the paint mixer will be able to mix colours similar to the suggested colours. Of course you don't have to use these colours, choose colours that are appropriate for your home and your lifestyle.

If you prefer another colour combination, first look at paint charts. With the wide range of colours available today, you may well be able to find the base-coat colour you want ready-mixed.

If not, you can buy a small amount of the colour closest to what you'd like and lighten, darken, or otherwise alter it with artists' oil paints or universal stainers, which are affordable and easy to use, available in many colours, and compatible with oil- and water-based paints. When you get the colour you want, you can paint a sample on a board, take it to the paint shop, get the colour matched, and have larger quantities mixed.

Before you apply your base coat, refer to Chapter Three, *Preparing to Paint*, for complete instructions.

## EXPERIMENTING WITH SAMPLES

Before going any further, base-coat several sample boards in the colour you plan to use for your technique so that you can test your glaze on them and get a true impression of what your finished effect will look like.

Paint samples on double-ply, hot-press illustration board available from art shops. These have a particularly smooth surface. Use boards about 60 x 80cm so that you get a good preview of your finished effect. Prime the boards so that they won't bubble and will absorb paint in the same way as your surface. Use the type of primer (oil-based, emulsion, or shellac) that is compatible with your base coat (see chart, Chapter Three).

# Glazes

In this book, many of the "oil-system" finishes (those executed in oil-based paints) feature a true "glaze" over their base coats—a glaze being distinguished from paint by its transparent quality, which comes from combining paint with glazing medium and solvent.

Some of the oil-system finishes and all the "water-system" finishes shown, however, don't use any glazing medium at all. Over their base coats are either paint applied straight from the can or paint mixed with the appropriate solvent.

Your first step in mixing a glaze should be to read the recipe for the decorative finish you want to create. Check the recipe chart to find out if you need water- or oil-based glaze or paint, referred to on the chart as an "Applied Finish". Decide if you want to replicate the colour in the book or devise one of your own. As with your base coat, if you want to get the exact colour of paint (whether used in glazing liquid or alone) in the recipe, you can take the book to a shop that sells mix-to-order paints and match the colour up to their charts.

A recipe for mixing an oil-based glaze follows. For water-system finishes, instructions for getting paint to the desired consistency using water are noted in the recipe.

Keep in mind, however, that just as in cooking, recipes for glazes are general guides. In cooking, you follow the steps, taking into account variations in, say, cooking time because of oven temperatures and the type of food being prepared. Mixing a glaze is somewhat similar; the process must be adapted to the needs of each technique or surface. Some techniques demand a very translucent glaze; others work best with pure paint. Some surfaces are best served by a thick glaze that won't run.

Because of these variations, you should always read the complete recipe and its chapter introduction before mixing a glaze. That's where you'll find clues to proper consistency and translucence.

Testing, however, is the only way to be sure you've got what you need. The best way to test is to apply glaze over a sample board painted with your base coat (see "Experimenting with Samples", above).

Even with testing, problems can crop up. If your glaze doesn't cover your surface well enough or you find it running, don't panic. First, wipe it off with a clean cloth. Then, only if needed, wipe surface with a cloth dampened with thinner.

There is a counterpart to transparent oil glaze for the water-based system, which you might want to try. It is transparent acrylic gel medium, which you mix with water and tint with artist's acrylics or universal stainers. (You can find instructions for mixing acrylic glaze in the first edition of *Recipes for Surfaces*, page 82.)

## MIXING AN OIL-BASED GLAZE

**M**ixing a glaze is simple. And there's a simple way to tell if you have got it right. Start by mixing up a batch of standard proportions (see p. 28). Then dip a brush into it, and swipe it across a piece of newspaper. If you can read the print through the glaze, you've got a good level of transparency.

Next, check your glaze's consistency. Ideally on a sample board painted with your base-coat colour, but even on plain white paper, use some of the glaze to make imprints with the tool employed in creating your finish (i.e., sponge, rag, comb, etc.). If the imprint is too thick, thin the glaze with white spirit. But be sure to add just a little at a time, and test as you go. (The thinner will, of course, also make the glaze more translucent.)

Going slow is very important because it's pretty tough to thicken a glaze you've thinned too much. With a small batch of glaze, it's probably best to mix a new batch. For a large amount, you can let it stand open to the air for about 12 hours until most of its solvent evaporates. A skin may form on top of the glaze as it thickens, in which case strain it through cheesecloth to remove the skin. Here are the materials you'll need:

- newspaper or dust sheet to cover your work surface
- rubber gloves
- mask
- newspaper on which to test glaze for transparency; household paint brush about 5cm wide to test glaze
- plastic container to hold glaze
- paint stirrer
- transparent oil glaze
- oil-based paint such as artists' oil or universal stainers

Also have ready: the tool you'll use to apply the glaze for the finish you've chosen; white spirit to further dilute your glaze, as needed; and the tool you'll use for your finish so that you can test the imprint it gives you.

Note that white spirit isn't the only thinner you can use with oil-based glaze:

- flatting oil, a mix of turpentine, linseed oil, and dryer specially formulated for compatibility with ready-mixed glazes
- turpentine, which causes glazes to dry more slowly than white spirit does (thus, giving you more time to work a surface)

The step-by-step photographs show how to mix a small batch. For the amount of glaze needed for a larger project, see Chapter Two, *Paints and Tools*.

---

**Important Note:** if you use artists' oil paints to tint transparent oil glaze, mix the paint to a smooth consistency with white spirit before adding it to your glaze. You will need to squeeze about 9cm of paint from the tube, to 0.5 l of oil glaze. If you do not dissolve the paint first in this way, you will find that the small particles of oil paint will cause large streaks when you come to paint.

## Mixing an Oil-Based Glaze: Step-by-Step

1. Open transparent oil and mix well; product tends to separate. Pour glaze into container and tint with universal stainers. or artists' oils. (See note at bottom of page 62.)

2. Test transparency by painting it over newsprint; if you can read print, glaze is transparent enough. Also test the consistency by applying it with tool you'll use for your technique and evaluating the imprint. Add white spirit, if needed, a little at a time. Test after each addition. Don't exceed one-third of mixture.

GENERAL INFORMATION

CHAPTER FIVE

# BEFORE YOU BEGIN

If you're thinking about diving right in without going through the rest of the book, please at least take just a few minutes to read these pointers before starting your decorative-painting project. It'll save you time, money, and lots of aggravation—while making your painting experience much more fun and your results much more professional. We promise!

*Practise . . . please!* More than anything, this is what will give you a professional look. It's also the key to making this creative undertaking a pleasure instead of a strain.

We're not talking long-term commitment here—but the first time you try a technique shouldn't be on your walls. Of course, you can paint over a finish if you're not satisfied with it—that's one of the pluses of decorative painting.

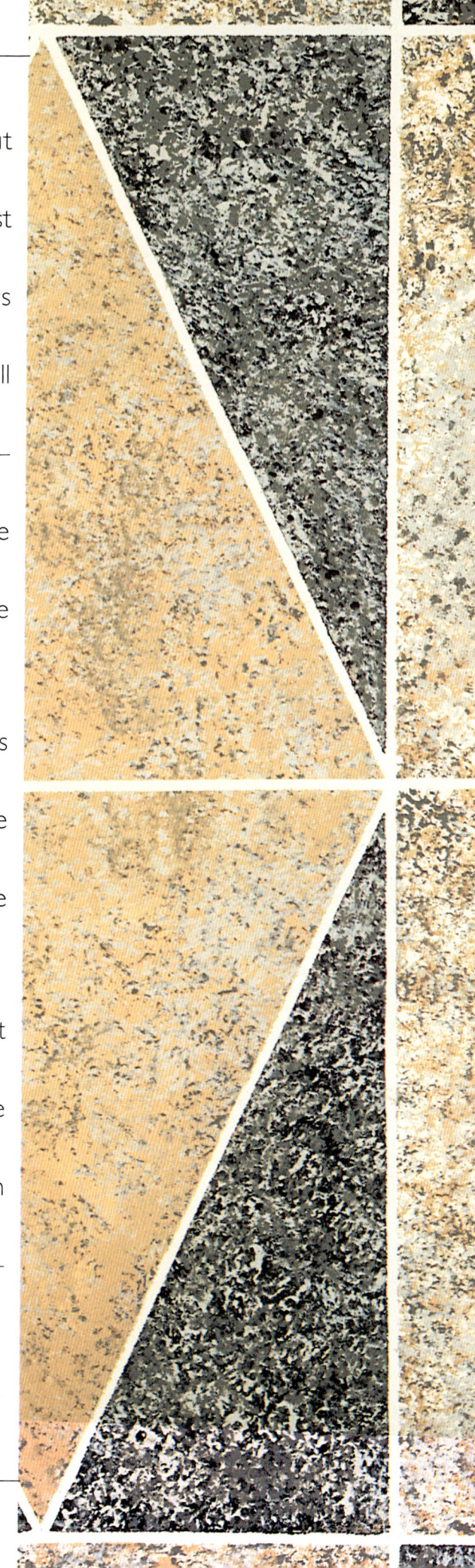

But why waste the time and materials, when a few dry runs on cardboard will let you find out such things as:

- if you really like the colours you've chosen when you see them one on top of the other in their final form ("textured" glaze over base coat)

- if the glaze you've mixed is opaque enough to give you a true decorative painting effect

- just how much pressure to use in applying paint to get the looks you see in the following pages

- just how much paint to apply to your surface to get the look you want

**EXPERIMENT!** While you're practicing, experiment with everything, especially colour. Just consider the colours of the finishes you see in these pages "serving suggestions". Specially selected for their ability to work with today's most popular decorating schemes, these hues are fashionable in home furnishings and accessories, even ready-to-wear.

But the key is not to let the colour a finish appears here limit you and your decorating schemes. This book is just a guide. Perhaps a lighter, darker, or whole new shade would better suit your decor. Don't hesitate to add your own creative input. For inspiration and instruction, see the chapters on *Colour* and *Mixing Paints* in this book.

**KEEP IT CLEAN!** Remember that "foreign particles"—dirt, dust, bristles from brushes, fuzz from cloth rollers—are the enemy of decorative painting. Keeping these elements off your finishes is also crucial to getting a professional look. One good tip: use foam rollers and brushes instead of cloth rollers and bristle brushes so that you don't end up with fuzz and hairs in your finishes.

Also: make sure your work environment is clean. Do the preparatory work—wash down your surfaces, smooth them out, etc.—and then clean up thoroughly, especially after sanding.

**WATCH HOW YOU WORK IN PAIRS!** Some techniques—the "subtractive" one in which you apply glaze with a roller or brush and then remove it with a tool like a sponge or comb while it's still wet—are more easily executed by two, especially over a large area. But make sure each person keeps doing "the same job" all through the project.

In other words, if you start by rolling on the glaze, and your partner follows behind removing it with a cloth, don't switch in mid-stream. Your decorative painting style is like your signature—unique to you. The amount of pressure you use when you remove glaze, the way you hold the cloth, all make an impact on the final look of the finish. By switching, you'll end up with two styles on one surface.

**READ THAT RECIPE!** Before you begin, read the entire recipe for a technique, as well as the introduction to the chapter. You'll find additional colour suggestions, tips to make the project easier, and help in correcting results you might not be satisfied with.

As in cooking, be sure you have everything you'll need on hand. Reading the whole recipe first will give you a clear idea of what's needed and how you'll use it so that you can determine quantities for a particular project. A thorough reading will also help you work out how much time to set aside to complete the recipe.

BEFORE YOU BEGIN

## PAINTING POINTERS

**HOW BASE COATS WERE APPLIED** Almost all the base coats in this book have been applied with a roller, using traditional house-painting methods. (Exceptions include the chair and other small objects on which the base coat was either applied with a brush or sprayed on.)

For all the finishes, the base coat must be dry before glaze is applied. Drying times vary; see Chapter Two, *Paints and Tools* for guidelines. *Note that, in most cases, the recipes start at the point where you have a dry base coat and are ready to apply your glaze.*

**HOW GLAZES WERE APPLIED** With "subtractive" finishes (those that involve removing glaze), glaze has usually been applied with a roller. In some instances, however, it was applied with a brush to give the finish added texture or "direction". Note that brush size depends on the size of your project. For example, to glaze a wall in a reasonable amount of time, you'll want to use a brush 10cm wide or larger.

**HOW TO GLAZE IN CORNERS** One of your biggest challenge spots will be in the corners of a room. Excess glaze tends to gather in corners. You can dab some out with a brush or a sponge cut to fit. Dab each spot once, and wipe your tool on a clean cloth every few times.

Your best bet, however, is to paint your walls in this manner: opposite walls one day, then let them dry overnight. The next day, tape their edges, and paint the two remaining walls.

See the drawings at the right for the most effective way to glaze a room, as well as how to glaze a wall for both additive and subtractive techniques.

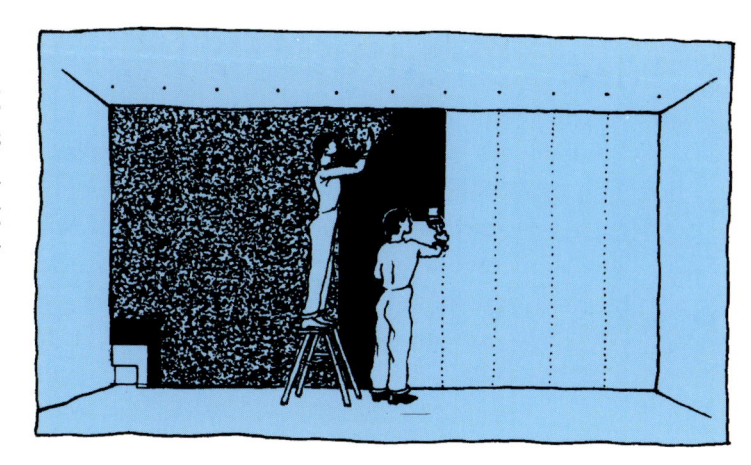

**Diagram shows how to glaze using a subtractive technique. One person begins rolling glaze from a top corner (left for right-handed, right for left-handed), working in a 60–90cm-wide strip. After reaching bottom of wall, this person returns to top of wall and begins glazing strip next to it, while other person manipulates wet glaze on first strip.**

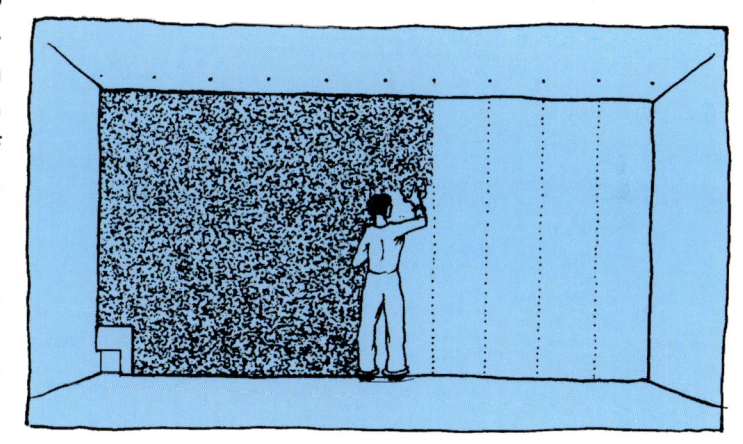

**Diagram shows how to apply glaze using an additive technique. Start in a top corner—left one if you're right-handed, right if you're left-handed so that your arm doesn't touch completed work. Move down wall in 60–90cm-wide strip; then go to top of wall and begin new strip next to it. Overlap strips just enough to avoid leaving a space where base coat shows through, but not enough to form dark line between rows.**

GENERAL INFORMATION

# MASKING

Speaking of tricks to make your life easier, masking is definitely one of them. Using tape to block out areas you don't want paint to get in can go a long way toward helping you achieve professional results. It will keep your work neat; give you clean-edged painted lines that go exactly where you want them to go; and make the classic technique of lining much easier to execute.

Following are examples from the recipes in this book where masking came in handy. Taping the skirting boards before rolling glaze over your faux-flagstone floor finish will keep them paint free while letting you get paint coverage right up to the wall edge. Taped lines form the mortar in the "Brick" recipe and create the inlay patterns in the "Granite" and "Malachite" recipes. Taping every other strip lets you grain more easily in the "Moiré" recipe.

Equipment-wise, you'll need scissors, masking tape, and a plastic spoon or a credit card. The latter is something you can use to rub the edges of the tape firmly into place—a very important step, and not one to skimp on. If the tape isn't sealed in place, paint could seep under the tape. In fact, even with extensive pressing, this is bound to happen at times. For this reason, you should always keep some of your base coat paint on hand for touch-ups. Using a small, fine artist's brush, you can carefully paint over any drips. You can also use paint thinner for oil paint or methylated spirits for emulsion paints on a cotton swab to remove any seepage.

Masking tape comes in many widths, from as narrow as 3mm, which might be just right for an inlay pattern, to as wide as 7.5cm, which could cover over moulding. It also comes in several levels of tackiness. For masking, look for "low-tack" or "safe-release" type tapes. These are less sticky and, thus, safer on already painted surfaces. You want a tape tacky enough to keep paint from seeping under, yet easy enough to remove—even after an extended period—so that it wouldn't, say, take the paint off your newly painted mouldings. Always test tape in an inconspicuous place first to prevent surprises.

## MASKING AN OBJECT

This clock is being prepared for painting with the "Malachite" recipe. You can see the finished version on page 99—if you had to hand-paint a circle around the face of the clock without getting any on the glass, it would certainly change the skill level required for this project. Masking in a circle keeps the project simple. Note that you must use a low-tack masking tape to cover the face of the clock.

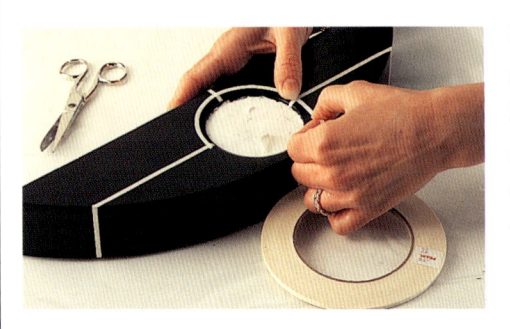

**Using 3mm tape, divide surface into sections to form inlay pattern. Align horizontal lines with base of clock. Make sure the tape is pressed firmly onto the surface with a plastic spoon or credit card so that no paint seeps underneath.**

BEFORE YOU BEGIN

# KEY WORDS TO KNOW

**Additive techniques:** One-person techniques in which you make impressions with glaze on a base coat using various tools such as sponges, rags, and brushes. Among these techniques are sponging on and ragging on.

**Artist's acrylics:** Paints made from ground pigment bound with acrylic medium, a transparent gel. They dry quickly to a waterproof finish and can be thinned with water. In decorative painting, you can use them for such techniques as marbling and *trompe l'oeil*, as well as to tint emulsion base coats and water-based glazes.

**Base coat:** Opaque layers of emulsion or oil-based paint that dry to a durable finish. In decorative painting, glaze is applied over the base coat.

**Blending:** Toning down imprints left in glaze by an implement such as a sponge, brush, or cloth to achieve a softer effect or to combine different-coloured glazes on a surface. Done by touching the surface with a light, feathering motion.

**Cloth distressing:** Using materials such as cheesecloth or cotton rags to apply or remove glaze. The most common method of distressing the surface is with material bunched up in your hand, as in the techniques of ragging and cheeseclothing. Material can also be used rolled into a tube, as in rag rolling, or in long strips, as in "Plastic-Wrap Ragging Off".

**Combing:** Drawing a toothed instrument, such as a graining comb or cardboard with teeth cut into it, through wet glaze produces effects such as "Moiré" and naive wood graining.

**Composition:** In decorative painting, how the light and dark areas of a painted finish or the multiple imprints of your tools form on a surface. You don't want a huge dark spot in one corner of your surface, for instance, because it will distract the eye from the overall look.

**Crackle glazing:** A way to give painted surfaces the tiny cracks that come with age. Crackle glaze can be bought ready-made in paint or craft stores or mixed from glue size and other ingredients. Crackling occurs because a water-based product is applied over an oil-based product. This method is related to *craquelure* in which a water-based varnish is applied over an oil-based varnish.

**Criss-crossing:** Method of applying base coat and glazing smoothly and evenly over a surface. Should always be employed when applying glaze with a brush to minimize brush marks. Begin by painting or glazing from top to bottom, then, without picking up more paint or glaze, go over it from side to side and, finally, lightly from top to bottom until you eliminate brush marks.

**Cutting:** Diluting pure paint or glazing medium with a thinner such as water or white spirit to give it a more workable consistency.

**Dabbing:** Touching surface lightly and repeatedly with a painting tool in quick motions, creating smooth, even marks. You dab with a rag in ragging techniques, with a brush in stencilling techniques.

**Découpage:** The traditional technique of gluing cut-out shapes of paper or other material to a surface and then covering the surface with several coats of varnish.

**Dragging:** Technique best executed by two people (especially over large areas) in which one person applies glaze with a brush or roller and the other person removes some of the glaze by sweeping over it with a metal graining comb, piece of cardboard with a feathered edge, dry paint brush, or other tool.

**Dry brushing:** Working with a brush that is almost free of paint. Brush may pick up paint from one part of glazed surface and move it to another, as in the "Rusted Metal" technique.

GENERAL INFORMATION

## KEY WORDS TO KNOW

**Dryer:** Chemical found in ready-mixed oil-based paints that speeds drying time. Also, chemical liquids such as terebine or liquid dryer, which you can buy in paint shops, to speed drying time of oil-based paints. Dryer should be added to paint a few drops at a time.

**Emulsion:** Water-based interior house paint similar to acrylic. It dries quickly, has little odour, and is available in finishes from matt to silk. Water-based glosses are also available.

**Fade-away:** An effect featuring a gradual progression of a glaze colour from dark to light or vice versa; or from one colour to another. Fade-away can be particularly effective with stencilling.

**Fantasy colours:** Reproducing natural materials in colours not found in nature, as shown in the "Marble" recipes.

**Flogging:** A decorative painting technique in which you manipulate the glaze by striking your surface with a long-bristled brush. A special "flogging" brush with 12cm-long bristles is ideal for executing this technique, but it is costly; instead, you can use a household painting brush with the longest bristles you can find.

**Fresco:** The age-old art of painting on fresh, still-wet lime plaster using pigments mixed with water. It produces soft, subtle colours and a finish of great depth. The "Fresco" recipe in this book captures the feeling of a frescoed surface using a simple cloth-distressing technique instead of pigments and plaster.

**Glaze:** Oil- or water-based paint that is transparent because it contains much more transparent oil glaze or water (depending on type of paint) than pigment. With many of the techniques in this book, the glaze contains just 20 per cent paint. Because of this, when applied over a base coat, the glaze's transparency allows the base coat to show through.

**Inlay:** To decorate a surface by insetting thin layers of fine materials into it. In decorative painting, the "inlay" look is great for faux granite, marble, and malachite. With malachite, for instance, that's the way it's usually seen. Because you work in small sections, painting is easier—shorter distances to keep your hand steady over and the design looking the same. Masking out areas between inlays with tape keeps them free of unwanted paint.

**Marbling:** Decorative painting technique that lets you capture the look of marble.

**Moiré:** Silk, rayon, or other fabric with a wavy or watermarked pattern running through it. Chinese water silk is an excellent example, and the basis for the "Moiré" technique in this book.

**Natural flow:** Also referred to as the "direction" of a finish, it means generally heeding the overall natural line and pattern of the material you are reproducing, i.e., the way the veining runs in marble, the way water would flow over a piece of metal and wear paint away naturally.

**Oil-based paint:** Interior or exterior house paint that comprises a mix of resin and oil. Used today instead of purely oil-based paint because it dries faster. Modern paints contain no lead.

**Palette: 1)** A thin oval or rectangular board, or a tablet of disposable sheets, on which you mix small quantities of paint. A traditional palette has a hole in it through which you stick your thumb to hold it. You can, however, also use a paper plate as an inexpensive and readily available alternative to a palette. **2)** The group of colours you choose for your decorative finish or room scheme.

**Pigment:** Powder ground from natural or synthetic material that gives paint its colour.

**Primer:** Sealant that goes under the base coat to protect the raw surface, make it non-porous, and prevent humidity and dirt from seeping in. There are many types of primer—which you use depends on your surface material.

## KEY WORDS TO KNOW

**Sample board:** A surface on which to practise techniques, experiment with colours, and preview your final effects. Primed 60 x 80cm double-ply, hot-press illustration board is recommended. It has a very smooth surface and is available from art shops. (Note: This is in addition to the white paper you should have on hand to test imprints of your tools and final colours before they go on your surface.)

**Shellac:** Alcohol-based primer that dries fast. It comes in various finishes, including clear, white, and orange (button polish). "Knotting"—used for preventing resin bleeding from knots through subsequent layers of paint—is also made of shellac.

**Smoothing out:** Getting rid of brush marks or softening painted lines on a still-wet painted or glazed surface. Move a long, soft-haired brush appropriate for your paint type and project size over surface in soft, feathery motion.

**Spattering:** Creating a fine array of coloured dots on a base coat by various methods including "printing" them on as in the "Spattering" technique and flicking paint off the bristles of a brush.

**Sponging:** Applying or removing glaze by dabbing a sponge on a surface. One of the most easily mastered and most popular techniques itself, it is also used in marbling, stucco, and many other techniques.

**Stencil:** Design cut out of cardboard, acetate, or stencil paper. You can buy stencils ready-made or make your own.

**Stencilling:** Placing a cut-out design on a surface and applying paint through it with a sponge, stencilling (or other type of) brush, or even spray paint.

**Stippling:** Applying paint over a surface with a very light, "staccato" dabbing motion; also the name of a decorative-painting technique that creates a finish with a fine texture of dots on a surface through the light dabbing motion with a rectangular stippling brush.

**Stucco:** A finish composed of cement, sand, lime, and water for exteriors, and fine plaster for interiors. Stucco recipe uses "Sponging" technique to capture effect.

**Subtractive techniques:** Two-step techniques in which glaze is first applied to surface with brush or roller, then partially removed or moved with tools such as rags, sponges, and brushes.

**Texture:** In decorative painting, it is not a raised surface, but one that gives the appearance of three-dimensionality by layering glaze colours and applying them with tools that create "texturedlike" patterns.

**Thinners:** Solvents that dilute paint to workable consistency; e.g. white spirit for oil-based paints, water for water-based paints.

**Universal stainers:** Highly concentrated liquid pigment for colouring both oil- and water-based paints, used by professional house painters and decorative painters. Stainers contain no dryer and thus should never equal more than 10 per cent of total volume of your paint—otherwise, paint won't dry.

**Varnish:** Final transparent coating used to protect painted finishes. Varnish will determine sheen of finish. It comes in flat to high gloss; pick sheen most compatible with your finish.

**Veining:** Linear pattern of marble; in addition to using paint brush to simulate it, a feather makes a highly effective veining tool, as seen in "Red Marble" technique.

**Verdigris:** Appealing, and highly popular, greenish blue-grey finish that develops on copper, bronze, and brass as part of natural ageing and weathering processes.

**Working dry:** Applying thin layer of glaze, just enough to cover surface; or applying bit of pure paint (or paint to which just a little thinner, glazing medium, or water has been added) and working it across surface with brush, rag, or other tool.

**Working wet:** Applying a lot of glaze, often in several colours, one on top of the other before the previous one dries, so that you can blend colours right on your surface as you work. The effect can be seen in the "Flagstone" and "Rusted Metal" techniques.

GENERAL INFORMATION

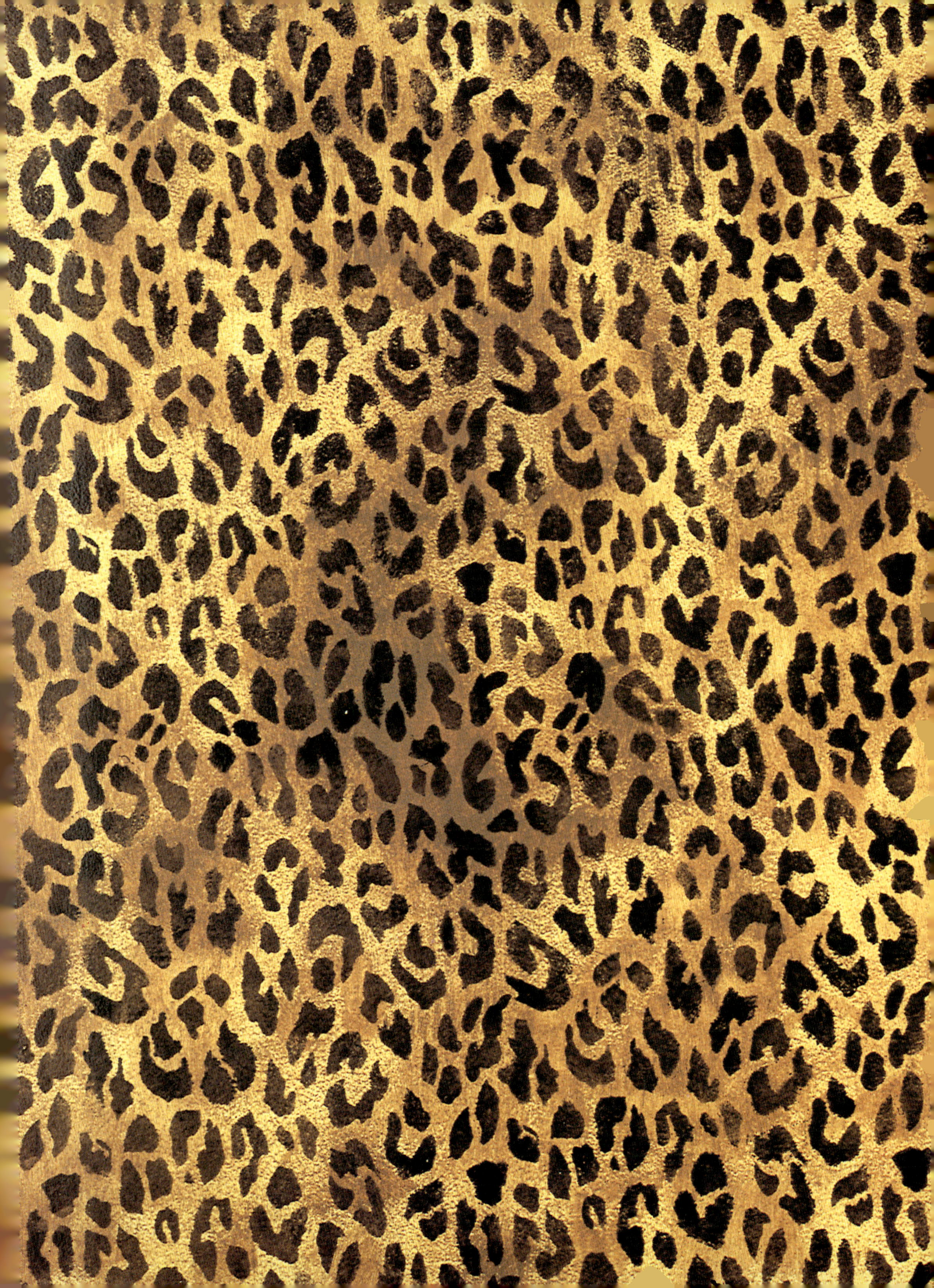

## Part Two

# THE RECIPES

# CHAPTER SIX

# METALS

The trio of techniques in this chapter are great for turning ordinary-looking or out-of-date objects into something special. The accessories you see on these pages were all either lucky finds or bought in junk shops. A change in colour was all it took to turn them into perfect complements to a wide range of room settings, or great gifts for special occasions, at a fraction of what they might cost in stores.

There are many more possibilities for including "ageing" metal in your decorating schemes than just on accessories. The rich colours of "rusted" metal are a great way to "highlight" the moulding in a room with a pale tone-on-tone "textured" wall finish, like those in Chapter Ten. Or, instead of boxing-in a hand basin to hide the pipes underneath, you might dress up those exposed pipes with an antiqued copper finish.

METALS

**Weathered-metal effects can work great decorative transformations on accent pieces as well as on less-expected elements of your home—like the pipes under your hand basin.**

If you have an old house and have been viewing those old freestanding metal radiators as eyesores, you might turn them into eye-catching decorative elements with the weathered-bronze effect. A beaten-up wooden bed frame, or a plain metal one, could easily be updated and become the centrepiece of a bedroom with any of these recipes.

And don't stop inside. Maybe you've just had the exterior of your house painted; if you have a wrought-iron railing out front, here's a way to refresh that, too. Even gutters and drain pipes are fair game. However, remember that if you use these metal recipes on outdoor surfaces, you must use paint that is compatible with the setting.

Consult your local DIY store to make sure your efforts won't crumble under an assault of sun, wind, and rain. And test first: oil paints sold for exterior use are often much glossier than the paint used here. The sheen won't make much visual sense on your carefully "aged" surface. You might instead be able to use an interior paint topped by a heavy-duty varnish—in which case you'll want a varnish with a matt finish.

However, for a realistic feel, have your brush marks mimic the way water would naturally move over your object—i.e., running down the sides, thus creating vertical streaks in the finish, and puddling up inside, forming a surface pitted in spots where the finish had worn away.

**Before you start your project, study real-life examples of weathered metals, such as the garden tap on this page. You'll see a great range in shades of colour and the patterns they form, which gives you great leeway in creating your own effect.**

**THE RECIPES**

# COPPER VERDIGRIS

## RECIPE

### COPPER VERDIGRIS

**LEVEL OF EXPERTISE:**

**RECOMMENDED ON:** Accessories, picture frames, bed frames, mouldings, wrought-iron railings

**NUMBER OF PEOPLE:** 1

**TOOLS:** Newspaper or dust sheet; face mask; rubber gloves; white spirit for clean up; rag for touch up; 2.5cm round brush; paper to test brush imprint on

**BASE COAT:** Metallic copper oil-based paint (Flat oil-based paint is more matt than eggshell and is available from specialist shops.)

**APPLIED FINISH:** Oil-based flat paint

- Sea blue
- Sea green

**VARNISH:** No

---

The ageing process is particularly kind to copper and bronze; years of exposure to the elements leave them with a patina of verdigris—that appealing greenish blue-grey finish so popular in home design today. These are some of the simplest finishes to reproduce—and some of the most rewarding because even the beginning decorative painter will be able to come close to the often high-priced verdigris pieces in stores.

This hammered-metal bowl was pulled from a scrap heap and given new life with this recipe. The process began with the application of two coats of oil-based copper-coloured paint. Then the "ageing" started: dabbing blue and green oil-based paints over top and bottom, with paint concentrated more in some spots than others, then coming back with dabs of copper in places to bring up the background colour again.

What makes this finish work so well is its mix of flat and shiny paints. To retain that flat-shiny contrast, and to keep the colours distinct, it's best to let each colour dry between applications; otherwise, you'll get a little too much blending.

Even though you're working with oil-based paints, letting the colours dry between applications will be less time-consuming than you think, because the copper paint has a lacquerlike quality that allows it to dry quickly. This fast-drying quality comes at a price, however: strong fumes. So be sure to wear a face mask and to work in a well-ventilated room (or outside, weather permitting).

**1.** Over copper-coloured base coat dip 2.5cm brush into sea blue paint.

**2.** Dab brush on paper until almost dry. Stipple paint on inside and outside of bowl randomly concentrating paint in spots. Let dry.

**3.** Dip round brush into sea green paint, and repeat step 2. Let dry.

**4.** Stipple some of copper base coat over green spots to bring up some of background colour.

METALS

COPPER VERDIGRIS

1

2

3

4

THE RECIPES

BRONZE VERDIGRIS

## RECIPE

### BRONZE VERDIGRIS

**LEVEL OF EXPERTISE:**

**RECOMMENDED ON:** Accessories, picture frames, bed frames, mouldings, wrought-iron railings

**NUMBER OF PEOPLE:** 1

**TOOLS:** Newspaper or dust sheet; face mask; rubber gloves; white spirit for clean up; rag for touch up; low-tack masking tape; 5cm foam brush for painting base coat; palette; 5cm bristle brush or old house-painting brush; four car-wash or regular household sponges; paper for off-loading excess paint

**BASE COAT:** Oil-based silk-finish bronze

**APPLIED FINISH:** Oil-based matt paints— 3 shades of green

◆ Verdigris green

◆ Sage green

◆ Pine green

**VARNISH:** No

A variation of the previous recipe, this one imitates verdigris on bronze—an effect you can easily see for yourself: just take a look at a photo of the Statue of Liberty.

The wood base and cardboard shade of the candlestick lamp accepted the treatment with equal grace. Done in oils, the finish adhered well to both materials.

To make sure you have the same success with your object, do your surface-preparation work thoroughly. Preparation is what makes all the other paint layers adhere well. Sand your object, if needed, and fill any chips or scratches. Then paint your object with the appropriate primer. (For details, see Chapter Three.)

Again, the combination of a shiny base coat and matt glaze coats makes the look. Note that varnish is an unwelcome addition because it can add an overall sheen to your "well-weathered" surface.

Even though sponges are your main tool in this recipe, it is considered a "dry-brush" technique because of the minuscule amount of paint you use to create it. (Stencilling is another example of a dry-brush technique; it requires about the same amount of paint as this finish.) For best success, use a light touch in applying it, and build the finish up slowly so that the colours don't all run together. That's how you get the depth.

Remember to follow the general direction of the ageing process on your piece: water would run down vertical parts, causing streaks, and pool on horizontal surfaces, which would pit. This directional quality is similar to that discussed in the marbling techniques; you don't need to be a slave to it, but it will add to the realism of your effect.

**1.** With low-tack masking tape, cover any areas on which you don't want to get paint (in this case, electrical parts, inside shade, edge of cord). Dab dry sponge into first green paint colour, then blot off excess on paper, and dab onto lamp. Don't squeeze sponge in your hand. Hold it lightly, parallel to the surface. Apply paint randomly to create light and dark spots. Leave some gaps, which will be filled in with rest of paint colours.

**2.** Repeat process with two other shades of green. Use brush to push paint into cracks and crevices. Let first colour dry before applying second colour. Even in oils, this should only take about a half-hour because of how little paint is used.

**3.** Reapply base coat colour in spots to bring up background.

**4.** Let dry. Remove masking tape. Do not varnish; sheen won't work with "aged effect".

METALS

BRONZE VERDIGRIS

1

2

3

4

**THE RECIPES**  81

# RUSTED METAL

## RECIPE

### RUSTED METAL

**LEVEL OF EXPERTISE:**

**RECOMMENDED ON:** Accessories, picture frames, bed frames, mouldings, wrought-iron railings

**NUMBER OF PEOPLE:** 1

**TOOLS:** Newspaper or dust sheet; face mask; rubber gloves; white spirit for clean up; rag for touch up; low-tack masking tape; 5cm foam brush for painting base coat; palette; 5cm bristle brush or old house-painting brush; 2cm bristle brush; four car-wash or regular household sponges; paper for off-loading excess paint

◆ **BASE COAT:** Walnut brown oil-based eggshell paint

**APPLIED FINISH:** Oil-based eggshell paint in 3 colours, plus gold leaf paint

◆ Rust

◆ Ebony brown

◆ Honey

◆ Liquid gold leaf paint (spray or brush)

**VARNISH:** No

---

1. With 5cm bristle brush, paint gold leaf paint over brown base coat. Do not try for even finish; streaky look is desired. Let dry completely.

2. With 2cm bristle brush, paint a few strips of brown paint, then rust paint, then gold leaf. Work wet—using an up-and-down motion, sometimes starting at top of planter and sometimes at bottom. Overlap your strokes so that some of the colours mix together (but not so they blend into one colour).

METALS

# RUSTED METAL

**3. Continue working your way around object, working in small sections several centimeters wide to keep control of the effect.**

**4. Smooth over finish with clean, dry brush. Do not over-blend. Finished effect will have naturally streaky look.**

Rust can be beautiful—as this metal planter shows. It has the same delicate feel and rich coloration as you might find in tortoiseshell.

The planter is the beneficiary of a blending technique that replicates the effect of rainwater running down the sides of a metal container and puddling inside.

The key here is that you're "working wet"—blending paint colours right on the piece as you go. This is one finish where a streaky look is highly desirable.

Keep in mind, too, however, that like the previous two recipes, this is also a dry-brush technique; so the goal is to use as little paint as possible. In fact, the only real liquid you should need comes from the gold leaf paint, which contains solvent.

You may, however, need to add a bit more white spirit to mix the colours to your liking; you can do this by dipping the clean, dry brush in white spirit (or special thinner recommended by the paint manufacturer) and applying it to your surface. If necessary, go back over your surface with some of the paint colours to keep the streaked effect.

Note: go easy on the walnut brown paint; it can make a piece too dark very fast. It's really the background colour and looks best as if peeking through.

**THE RECIPES**

# CHAPTER SEVEN

# STONE

Painted finishes let you capture the spirit of materials you might not otherwise be able to have in your home. For instance, stone can be expensive, because its weight makes transportation costs prohibitive. And weight can also make it unsuitable for your interior without extensive (and costly) shoring up of structural elements.

As with the recipes in the *Reasonable Replicas* chapter, you won't get total realism from these stone effects, but that needn't be the goal. These finishes deliver a more casual, folk-art style, much in keeping with today's preferences for both relaxed design and self-expression in decorating.

When thinking where these effects might work in your home, consider the character you can give a room by painting its floor.

Flagstones, natural stone walling, and granite make great options. In an entrance hall, for instance, you can turn the mood formal with a granite inlay-pattern. A flagstone floor in a conservatory can do its part to help bring the outdoors inside.

There is some simple freehand painting involved in some of these techniques. Studying stone patterns will easily give you the hang of the basic stone shapes. Don't try to be exact, and don't be concerned if you make a mistake. That's part of the beauty of decorative painting—if you make a mistake, you can just paint over it and start again.

Note, too, that much of the texture and depth you sense in these finishes *doesn't* come from hand painting; it comes from the tools you use to execute the techniques—sea sponges, newspaper, etc.—and how you apply or remove the glaze.

For a guide to getting floors ready to paint, see Chapter Three, *Preparing To Paint*. For floors in poor condition, paint can be an ideal remedy, as long as you prepare them properly by repairing, stripping, sanding, and priming them.

And remember that when painting a floor you must use the proper type of paint. Review the suggestions in the *Paints and Tools* chapter, and check with your local paint store. Specialist highly durable floor paint is most likely your best choice for the base coat, topped by an oil-based glaze.

You'll also want to apply several coats of varnish for flooring to protect your design. For stone finishes, varnishing is a plus on another level: it brings out the depth and colour of the effect and gives it a more genuine feel.

Keep in mind, too, that with floors you must plan to "paint yourself out of the room". You'll end up starting over, of course, if you have to walk over your newly painted finish before it dries.

# FLAGSTONE

## RECIPE

### FLAGSTONE

**LEVEL OF EXPERTISE:**

**RECOMMENDED ON:** Floors, fireplace walls, bath surrounds

**NOT RECOMMENDED ON:** Highly carved surfaces, small surfaces

**NUMBER OF PEOPLE:** 2 recommended, but can do with 1

**TOOLS:** Newspaper or dust sheets; roller (with extension handle, depending on project) to apply base coat and glaze; paint trays; paint stirrers; face mask; rubber gloves; masking tape to cover areas you don't want painted (like moulding); paint containers; paper to test colours on; chalk pencil or chalk to draw outlines of stones; medium-size rounded fitch brush; lightweight plastic sheeting (about 1mm), cut into wide strips somewhat larger than the size of your stones; car-wash sponge

◆ **BASE COAT:** Maize emulsion floor paint

**APPLIED FINISH:** 3 colours of emulsion floor paint thinned with water; plus transparent oil glaze and Payne's Grey artists' oil paint.

◆ Birch

◆ Charcoal

◆ Aubergine

◆ Glaze: Charcoal oil-based silk-finish interior house paint

**VARNISH:** Several coats required for floors

---

Right from the start, take our word for it: there's no one precise way of doing this finish. The basic idea is that you don't want two stones of the same colour next to each other. You avoid this by creating more colours from the three main paint colours used in the recipe right on your surface.

The colours you'll mix in advance are birch, charcoal, and aubergine. You'll need to mix a third shade of grey right on your surface by combining the two grey paints you already made up. Other shades will be a natural offshoot of "working wet". This means no waiting for paint to dry, or even cleaning your brush, between stone colours—in fact, it's the mixing as you go that gives the depth and richness—and makes you feel especially creative in the process.

In addition to the three colours already mentioned, you may also want to premix brick-red and grey-green colours, shades flagstone often comes in. Or, for a "slate" look, you can execute the technique solely in gradations of grey. And there's always the option of "fantasy" colours geared more to your decor than nature.

With this finish, colours *should* be streaky. That's what gives you the uneven character of the natural stone. But the outlines of the stones should be as neat as possible to give your stones the sharp edges typical of the real thing.

If you're working on a floor, first read the tips in the introduction to this chapter on what kinds of paint to use and what to watch out for. One especially crucial point is to check that the glazing liquid used for your final paint coat is suitable for floors—some are, and some aren't. In any case, you'll need to apply several coats of varnish over your finish to ensure long life on this high-use surface.

**Before you start on the stone finishes in this chapter, take some time to study the shapes, sizes, and colours of the stones found in really old structures like those on page 86.**

THE RECIPES

# FLAGSTONE

1. Draw stone shapes on floor with chalk pencil; if you need to make a change, wipe off chalk line with cloth. Then, plan colour arrangement so that no two stones of same colour are next to one another. Write colour name—charcoal, birch, aubergine, etc.— inside outline of each stone.

2. Pour three paints into containers. Note that on a floor, you can't paint all stones of one colour first, or you'll eventually have to walk over wet work. Paint in sections. With fitch brush, outline first stone in birch, then fill in. Off-load some paint from brush onto next stone you'll paint, and even next few after that. (The mix with the colour you plan to paint those stones will give each stone a unique coloration.)

3. Dip brush into charcoal paint, and paint over second stone (streaks of birch already on it). Stroke some charcoal on first stone you painted, as well as some nearby stones, and work colours while wet to get streaky look.

4. Paint next stone with aubergine, following steps 2 and 3. Continue over surface, using this colour to form new shades on stones you've already painted as well as stones you have yet to paint.

5. Working with all three colours, complete one section at a time. Let dry thoroughly.

6. With roller, apply charcoal glaze in criss-cross motion over small section of surface (as far as you can reach—you can not walk over wet glaze to complete technique). Glaze, 80/20 mix of glazing liquid and paint thinned with white spirit, should be transparent enough to see stones through well.

7. Roughly accordion-fold wide plastic strip to crease it, and smooth it down over a stone. Pull off.

8. Immediately dab around edges of stone with a sponge to blend it in and give area in between the texture of cement. Then move on to next stone in section, working fast while glaze is still wet. You can use same strip several times. (Note: working with a partner can make this easier.) Work section by section, over entire surface. Let dry.

STONE

FLAGSTONE

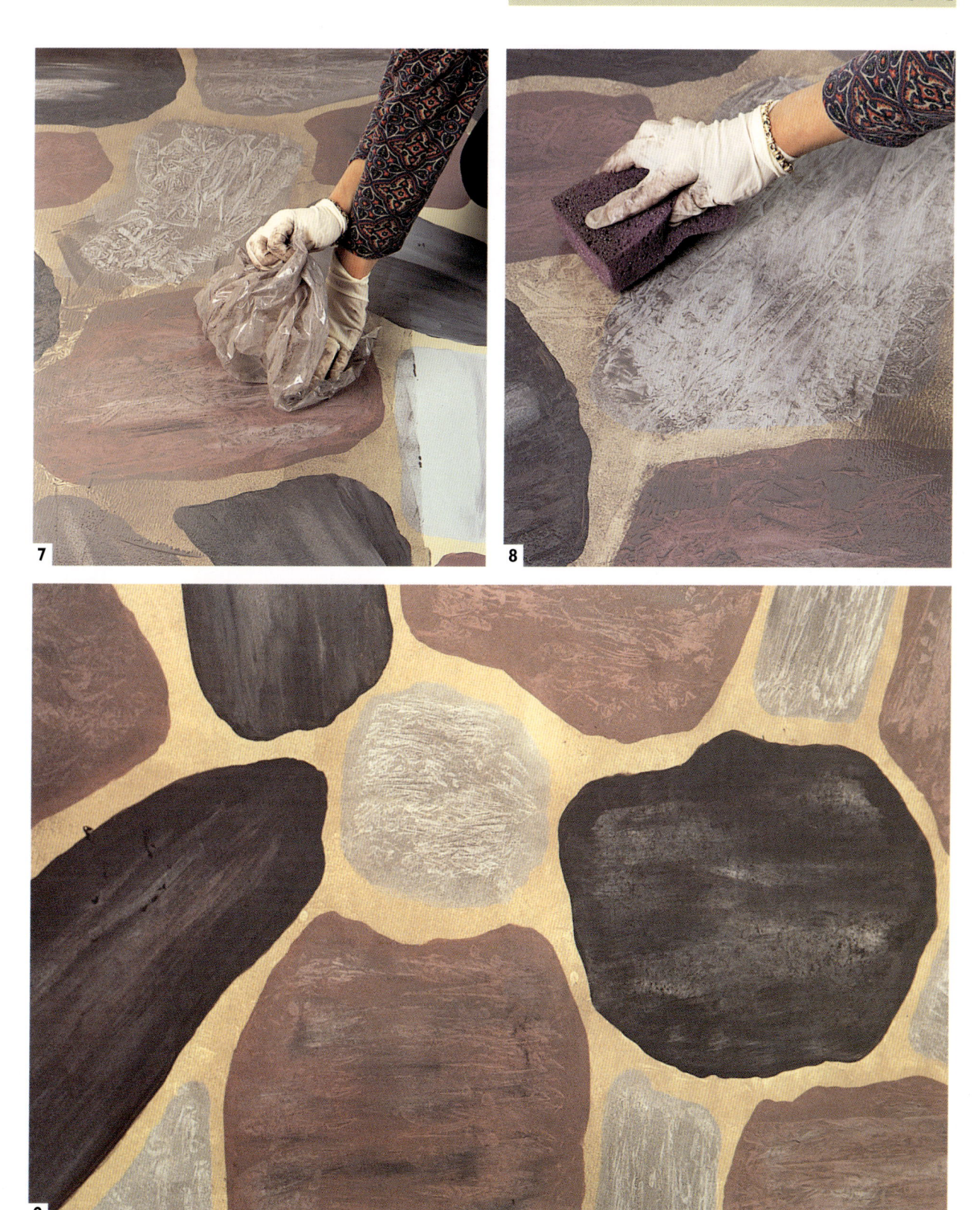

9. Apply several coats of varnish, per instructions on page 95.

THE RECIPES

STONE-WORK

## RECIPE

### STONE-WORK

**LEVEL OF EXPERTISE:**

**RECOMMENDED ON:** Floors, fireplace walls, bath surrounds

**NOT RECOMMENDED ON:** Highly carved surfaces, small surfaces

**NUMBER OF PEOPLE:** 2 recommended, but can do with 1

**TOOLS:** Newspaper or dust sheets; rubber gloves; paint tray; paint roller to apply base coat; newspaper ripped into sizes similar to your stones; 2.5cm rounded fitch paint brush; sea sponge; varnishing pad

◇ **BASE COAT:** Dove white matt emulsion paint (or floor paint)

◆ **APPLIED FINISH:** 2 oil-based eggshell paints

◆ Straw

◆ Ash

**VARNISH:** Required for floors

**One of the many colours and patterns of stone-work—study the shapes, then do your own freehand version.**

With this recipe, it's okay to use just one brush that you don't clean between colours and "contaminate" your paint; allowing the colours to blend together for a slightly dirty effect only adds to the finish.

Like the "Flagstone" and "Granite" finishes in this chapter, and the "Brick" finish in Chapter Nine, faux stone-work would make great flooring in a conservatory, porch, utility room, or kitchen. If you'll be working on a floor, be sure to first see the notes in the introduction to this chapter on paints to use and what to watch for.

Don't be put off by the thought of painting in the stones freehand. Give your eye something to get a rough idea from, and you'll get them just fine. There's no need to be exact—there are so many colours and patterns of stone-work; a version like yours exists out there somewhere. And, as when painting the veining in the marbling techniques in Chapter Eight, or the details on the "Grape-Leaf Motif", the best advice is to stay loose. Don't agonize over every paint stroke. Have fun!

Another thing that might surprise you is how you get the "texture" and shading that gives the stones their 3-D look. There's no artistic shading involved; simply press newsprint over the wet glaze, lift off, and there it is. The texture comes from the varying amounts of glaze absorbed by the newsprint.

STONE

STONE-WORK

1. Over dry base coat, paint in stone shapes with fitch brush and straw paint. Work in sections, painting outline of each stone first, then filling in. Leave roughly the same amount of white space between the stones.

2. While paint is still wet, press newspaper over stone shapes and pull off to get textured imprint.

3. Paint ash paint over stones, outlining first and then filling in.

4. Press newspaper over each stone, then lift off.

5. Wet a sea sponge with water, and wring out. Dab sponge in straw paint. Sponge on in between stones, replenishing paint on sponge as needed, to blend edges and soften finish. If finished effect is desired on floor, apply several coats of varnish with paint pad. (See page 95 for varnishing instructions.) Finished effect is featured on opening pages of this chapter.

THE RECIPES

GRANITE

## RECIPE

### GRANITE

**LEVEL OF EXPERTISE:**

**RECOMMENDED ON:** Floors, panelling, columns

**NOT RECOMMENDED ON:** Highly carved surfaces

**NUMBER OF PEOPLE:** 1

**TOOLS:** Newspapers or dust sheets; rubber gloves; paint roller to apply base coat; paint tray; paint stirrers; graph paper, ruler, and coloured pencils or markers to create colour diagram of design; pencil; straight edge; spirit level; 12mm masking tape; foam brushes geared to size of project; 3 paint containers; small sea sponge; large sea sponge; paint pad for varnishing

**BASE COAT:** Dove white satin-finish emulsion paint

**APPLIED FINISH:** 4 emulsion paint colours

◆ Taupe

◆ Chalk

◆ Tawny

◆ Midnight grey

**VARNISH:** Use water-based varnish

---

Knowing how to sponge on can get you far in the world of decorative painting. Here it helps to create a mosaic of inlaid granite that could easily lend a bit of grandeur to an unimposing entry hall. (For more tips on sponging on, turn to the "Marbling" recipes, or the "Stucco" recipe. For a detailed guide to sponging, see the first edition of *Recipes for Surfaces*, page 91.)

You can create a pattern like the one you see, which employs a simple chequerboard effect of grey and chalk rectangles, centered by a tawny diamond. Masking tape over the base coat masks out the lines that divide the granite slabs, in much the same way it forms the "mortar" in the "Brick" recipe.

For divine pattern inspiration, check the floors in both old public buildings and modern shopping malls. Granite and its look-alikes can be found in a variety of settings these days. The colours you choose can be either true-to-life or "fantasy".

This finish uses more paint than many of the decorative effects you see in this book. It also employs two sponges instead of the usual one—which, in addition to changing the position of the sponge in your hand frequently, is a good way to get greater variation in your impressions. Here, the larger sponge makes an even overall pattern, while the smaller sponge leaves a more clearly defined "printed" mark on the surface.

With stone finishes, varnishing is a big plus because it brings out the depth and colour of the effect and gives it a more genuine feel. But, with this particular finish—and any finish that has white areas—be careful which varnish you choose. Whenever you use varnish over white paint, you run the risk of the paint yellowing. Look for a "non-yellowing" formula; but don't take the label at face value. Be sure to test the varnish on a practise surface first (however, it can take several months to yellow fully).

To begin the technique, apply white base coat with a roller. Let dry. Measure your surface, and then, on graph paper, draw a small colour diagram of your granite design to scale.

GRANITE

Sponging lets you reproduce the mottled surface of granite, shown above in an inlaid pattern.

1. Reproduce diagram full size, drawing lines lightly over base coat with pencil and straight edge. With level, check that lines are straight. Apply masking tape next to pencil lines, pressing firmly in place to prevent paint seepage. (That way, you'll paint over the pencil lines and won't have to worry about removing them.)

2. With foam brush, apply tawny paint to triangle. Let dry.

**THE RECIPES**

93

GRANITE

3

4

5

STONE

GRANITE

3. With foam brush, apply midnight grey to triangles, adjoining tawny triangle, and to adjacent rectangles in chequerboard fashion. Let dry.

4. Wet sea sponges with water and wring out until damp. Fill containers with tawny, taupe, and midnight grey paint. "Sponge on" over surface. With small sponge, apply taupe paint to entire surface, then tawny paint over white areas only. Paint dries quickly between coats because it's emulsion and you use so little of it.

5. With large sponge, apply midnight grey paint over entire surface. Let dry.

6. Remove masking tape. Apply two coats of water-based varnish with paint pad. Dip pad into varnish in paint tray. Hold pad flat against surface. Pull pad across surface in single swipes. Don't go back over areas just coated; you'll get any spots you missed with second coat. Let first coat dry before applying second (about 2 to 3 hours).

7. This finish illustrates how much your tools can influence your results. Imprints from two sponges contribute to the look, enhancing the sense of depth.

THE RECIPES

MALACHITE

## RECIPE

### MALACHITE

**LEVEL OF EXPERTISE:**

**RECOMMENDED ON:** Accessories, small surfaces such as tabletops

**NOT RECOMMENDED ON:** Highly carved surfaces

**NUMBER OF PEOPLE:** 1

**TOOLS:** Newspapers or dust sheets; face mask; rubber gloves; paint roller or household brush for applying base coat; paint tray; white spirit; paint stirrers; paper for testing effect on; cardboard, several pieces cut to size of your design's biggest shape; 3mm or 6mm masking tape, depending on project size; 2.5cm foam brush; small, flat bristle brush; cotton rags or paper towels; paint pad to apply varnish

◆ **BASE COAT:** Clover silk-finish emulsion paint

◆ **GLAZE:** Oil-based glazing liquid and spruce satin oil-based paint

**VARNISH:** Use oil-based varnish

**The rich colours and detailed patterns of malachite can be seen in the inlaid edge of this table.**

Great expanses of malachite are rare. What you see most often are malachite inlays, like the pattern created here. You can copy or adapt it, or create your own design, depending on the space or object to be painted. You might prefer a simpler design of just squares or rectangles. Or, you might come across an inlay pattern that appeals to you.

Working in smaller sections also makes the technique much easier. In any case, practise will be a big help—you want to feel confident in using your tool and in making the two kinds of marks that characterize malachite: "waves" and "centres".

This recipe employs a version of a decorative painting technique called "dragging". The technique can be challenging when done over great distances—say, from the top to bottom of a wall—but is much easier to master when done in short sections, as seen here. For one thing, if you don't like the way a section comes out, you can just paint over it and drag it again, without interfering with the rest of your design.

For this technique, you'll make your own tool from a piece of cardboard. *Neatly* rip the cardboard into small rectangles the width of the widest shape in your design. How you rip the cardboard is crucial. You don't want to cut it with scissors because you want a feathered edge. But you must tear

MALACHITE

it very carefully so that you don't get any extra-big gaps in the cardboard that would let too much glaze through and mess up the malachite pattern. Make sure you test each tool you make to be sure you like the impression it creates.

When you drag the wavy sections, start at the top of a shape and decide which way you want the pattern to go. For the "centres", use a small, flat bristle brush and swirl it slightly, pushing it into the glaze so that it forms the lines. Place one centre directly adjacent to the next.

Dragging also plays a major part in the recipe for "Sedimentary-Style Marble"; you use the same tool. See page 110 for more tips.

The deep, rich greens of malachite make for an eye-catching finish, but they don't have to limit your colour choices. As in the *"Fantasy" Marbling* chapter, you can do this technique in nonconventional colours, as well. However, you may find tone-on-tone combinations most appealing because they offer the least distraction from malachite's distinctive pattern.

This finish looks particularly wonderful on small objects—where you most often see real malachite. To get a sense of the malachite effect small-scale, in 3-D, study the photo of the clock on page 99. (See the section on "Masking", page 68, for tips on preparing the clock for painting.)

**1. Measure your surface, then, on graph paper, draw diagram "to scale" (i.e., in proportion to your room) of inlay pattern you want. Then draw full-size pattern on surface, putting in lines lightly over base coat with pencil and straight edge. Check lines with level. Next, apply masking tape lines, pressing firmly to prevent paint seepage.**

**2. With foam brush, blot spruce glaze onto one small inlay section at a time. Paint all the way to edge and over tape.**

THE RECIPES 97

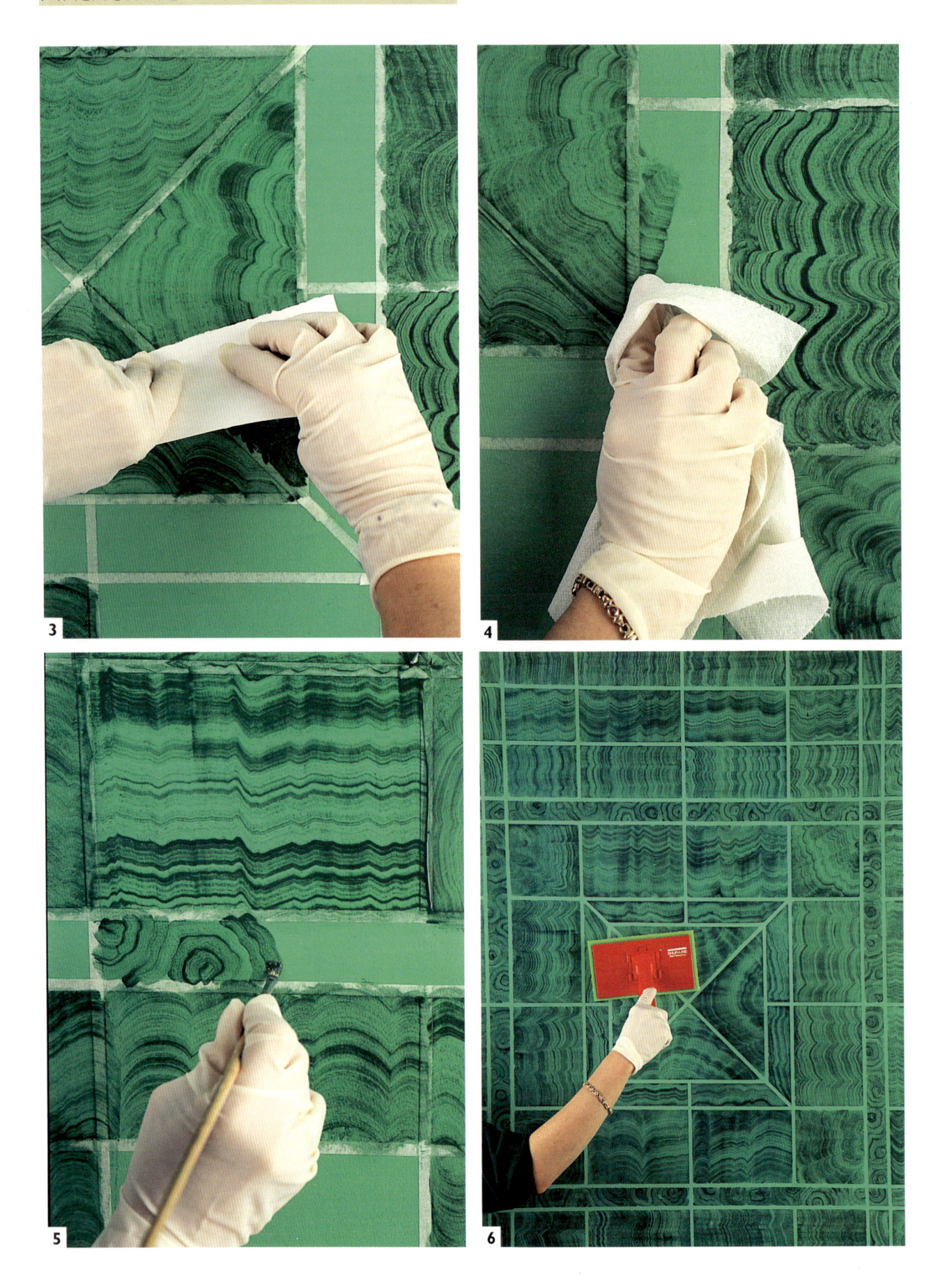

## MALACHITE

# MALACHITE

3. Immediately drag cardboard tool over glaze in that section before it dries. Use wavy motion, pressing firmly and holding cardboard at 45-degree angle. As you drag, stop briefly after each curve to form natural lines of malachite. Wipe tool on rag before starting next section. Paint and drag every other shape in your design, moving along in the same direction, then let those dry. Vary direction and pattern of your lines, as shown, making some semicircular rows and some bands of wavy lines.

4. Immediately clean up any glaze that runs over into next section with clean, dry cotton rag. Once "non-adjacent" sections have dried, you can tackle the rest of the shapes, one at a time, without smearing the work you've already done.

5. With small, flat bristle brush, paint semicircular-line pattern in remaining sections.

6. Remove tape. Apply two coats of varnish with small paint pad (See instructions on page 95.)

This simple wood clock was transformed with this recipe for malachite into a one-of-a-kind treasure.

**THE RECIPES**

# CHAPTER EIGHT

## "FANTASY" MARBLING

Marbling is everywhere today—you can find it on everything from sheet sets to photo frames to laminate countertops and vinyl flooring. And, most importantly, you can find it in many more colours than Mother Nature ever intended. Marbling in "fantasy" colours, often accented with metallics, abounds.

In this chapter, you'll find recipes for three imaginative examples—shimmering red, a sparkling blue, and a warm sedimentary-style marble in watercolour hues that conjure up Uluru at sunset.

Mastering marbling could take a lifetime—but it doesn't have to. So many of the marbleized effects you see today are just impressions of the real thing. Your own interpretation could easily be the best complement to your decorating scheme.

**Marble's translucence makes it an ideal subject for the decorative painter—the translucence is reproduced by layering paint and glaze. Note, too, the "directional quality" of marble, as seen in the photo above: veining all runs in the same general direction, like a school of fish.**

Note, however, that studying marble and really looking at the shapes that make up this spectacular stone are vital; the more time you put into looking, the more your work will benefit. The more you look, the more you'll see how many kinds of marble there are—travertine, brecciated, variegated, serpentine—and, thus, how many options you have.

Looking carefully will also help you understand the essence and structure of marble. Decorative painting has a crucial quality in common with marble—translucence. Some of marble's veins and colouring show through clearly on the surface; others appear only hazily. This same effect can be achieved by the layering effect of glazes over the base coat.

Marble's layered effect is a result of the way the stone forms: under pressure and through a natural heating and cooling process that forms the veins and fragmented layers, which eventually harden into solid stone.

Something else that will help you get the finish you want is practice. This is no general statement. There is a painterly quality to this technique; you need to experiment with artistic things like "composition", i.e., where you put those light and dark patches, which way you run the veining.

There is, however, a real key to doing this without going to art school: *think "fish"*.

Keeping an open mind, study the photo of real marble at left. Focus on the veining, and you'll see two things: **1)** The lines all flow pretty much in the same direction. Thus, when you do your marbling, choose a main direction to run the veins. **2)** The lines form irregular groups of diamond shapes reminiscent of schools of fish all swimming in the same direction. Keep making rough fish shapes (minus tails, of course), and you'll create a basic structure for your finish that "says" marble.

"Thinking fish" may also help you with another crucial task: staying loose. Don't go into it thinking, "Marbling is for professionals with years of experience. I've got to concentrate to get it right".

The key is in how you hold your brush when you paint your fish shapes: not like a pencil, but *loosely*, and *by the tip*. The looser you hold it, the more natural your lines will look. And the more lines and layers of colour you add, the more you get those feelings of movement and depth, which are the essence of real marble.

RED MARBLE

## RECIPE

### RED MARBLE

**LEVEL OF EXPERTISE:**

**RECOMMENDED ON:** Panelling, floors, mouldings, columns, tabletops, bath surrounds, fireplace mantels, furnishings, accessories

**NOT RECOMMENDED ON:** Highly carved surfaces

**NUMBER OF PEOPLE:** 1

**TOOLS:** Newspaper or dust sheets; face mask; rubber gloves; paint tray; paint stirrers; palette; large feathers; white spirit; 5cm foam paint brush for raspberry-coloured glaze; paint rollers for applying base coat and red glaze; plastic bags or plastic wrap; cotton rags about 30cm square; paint pad to apply varnish

**BASE COAT:** Melon silk-finish emulsion paint

**GLAZES:** Gold leaf oil-based transparent oil paint, plus glaze and 3 oil-based eggshell colours

Tomato

Raspberry

Plum

**VARNISH:** Use oil-based varnish

Although you'll get some seriously beautiful results with this technique, it'll be hard to take the *process* too seriously, considering the tools you use to execute it. What better way to create marble's feathery-edged veining than with a feather? And, instead of struggling with a brush, you can just use scrunched-up plastic bags to mask out those "fish" shapes so characteristic of marble.

For large surfaces, you'll need about five large feathers. You can buy them in fishing-supply stores and in art supply stores.

Your goal with this finish is to create a sense of depth. To do that, you must break up the surface visually. The gold veining, plus three other glaze colours, overlapped and applied in different manners, help you to do this. To capture the translucence of marble, the three glazes are thinned with enough white spirit so that the base coat and veining show through, augmenting the layered effect.

Stand back often as you work, and see where you need to darken a light area and vice versa, building up as you go. Always use just a little paint at a time, keeping a light touch and blending the colours. Use darker colours to create shadows around your fish shapes and, thus, give your finish a three-dimensional quality.

There's also a special trick to this finish: varnishing twice—once after painting the veining and once at the end. Why? Damage control. Say you've completed your veining. Now you varnish over it. Then, you put on your next glaze layer, and if you don't like the way it comes out, you can just wipe it off without removing your veining and having to start from scratch.

**THE RECIPES**

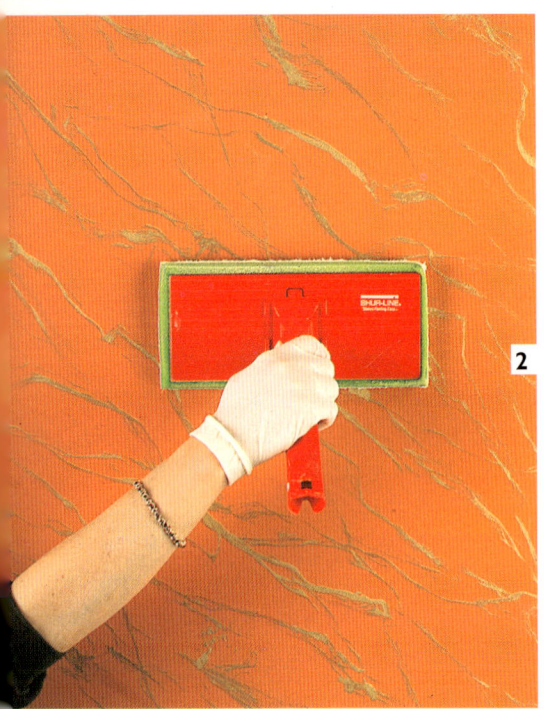

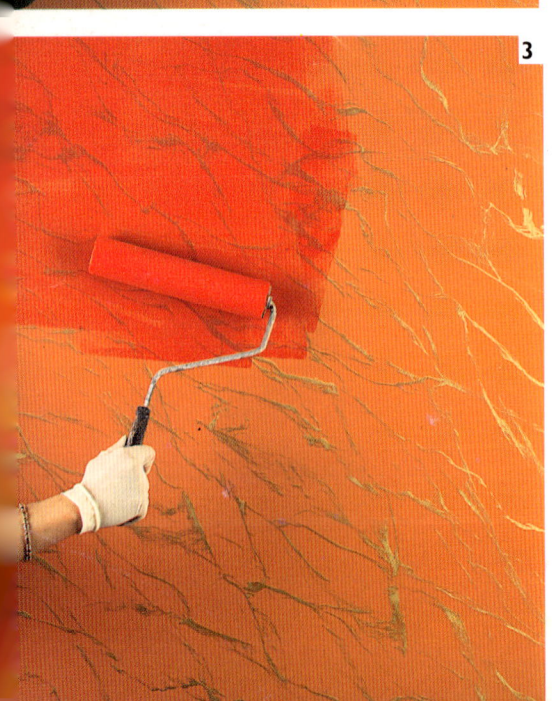

1. Pour gold leaf paint into paint tray. Dip top half of feather into paint. Holding feather loosely, run edge and tip downward over base coat, creating pattern of diamonds that looks like fish swimming in same direction. Overlap some "fish", and vary size. Rotate feather slightly by turning wrist as you paint to get thick and thin lines. Let veining dry thoroughly. Set gold paint aside; you'll use it again in step 8. Clean feather with paint thinner, wiping in feather's natural direction.

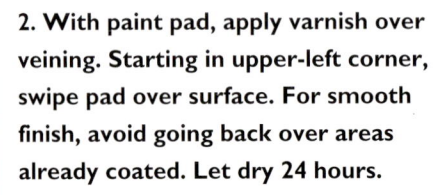

2. With paint pad, apply varnish over veining. Starting in upper-left corner, swipe pad over surface. For smooth finish, avoid going back over areas already coated. Let dry 24 hours.

3. Pour thin tomato glaze into a paint tray. Apply glaze in criss-cross motion with a roller. Glaze should be transparent enough to see veining and base coat. Set glaze aside; you'll use it again in step 9.

4. Press plastic bags firmly onto wall, shaping them into "fish". Arrange them on diagonal, following fish shapes you created with veining. Overlap some bags. Keep bags from getting square shape. Bags will stick to paint until you remove them. For entire wall, work in 1-2.4 m sections, starting in top corner. (Note: you will need a ladder.)

5. Using raspberry glaze and tip of 5cm foam brush, paint around plastic bags with loose, rough strokes.

6. Crumple wad of plastic wrap in your hand and dab raspberry glaze to blend it and give soft edge to fish shapes.

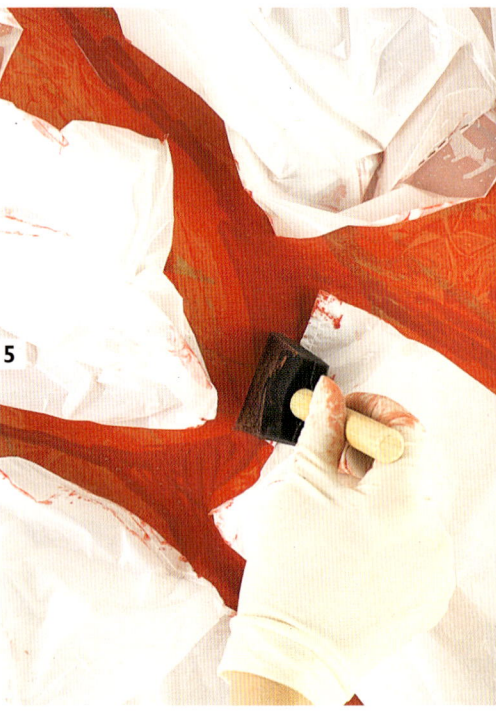

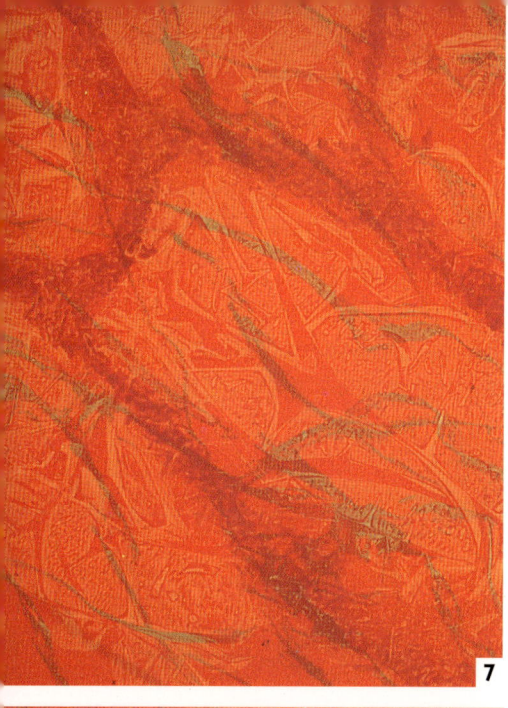

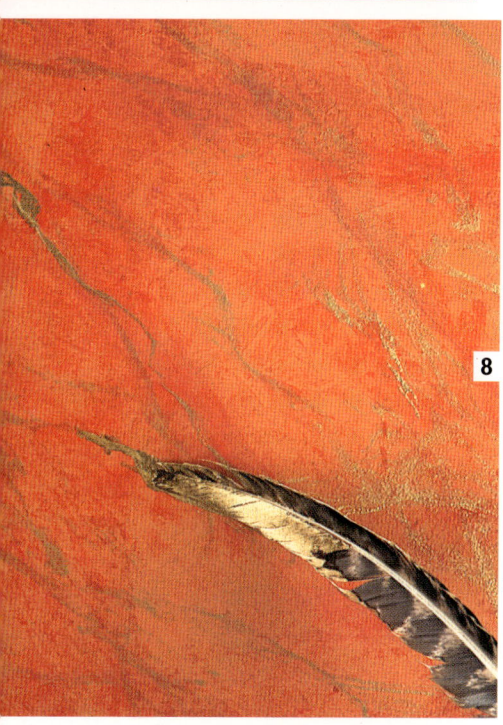

**7.** Remove plastic bags. Note that some raspberry glaze comes off with bags, leaving light imprints of crumbled plastic. Let glaze dry thoroughly.

**8.** With feather and gold paint, highlight alongside some of the veins. Vary length and placement of highlights—on top, sides, underneath. Follow bolder lines, working to break up surface further. Let dry.

**9.** With feather and tomato glaze, darken some areas, following the fish shapes you created. Don't outline the shapes; make V's. Stand back from your work often to see where you need more colour. Use a light touch so that you can still see your original gold veins. Let dry.

**10.** With cotton rag, apply plum glaze. (Note: glaze needn't be as thin as others because it is rubbed on.) Dab rag in glaze, dab off excess on paper— rag should be almost dry. Make streaky lines in same direction as your shapes, in some places roughly outlining shapes for 3-D effect. Apply paint lightly at first and build up, as needed, standing back to see where you can use more colour. (If you put on too much paint, just "rag" it off.) Let dry thoroughly.

**11.** For marblelike sheen, apply varnish as in step 2.

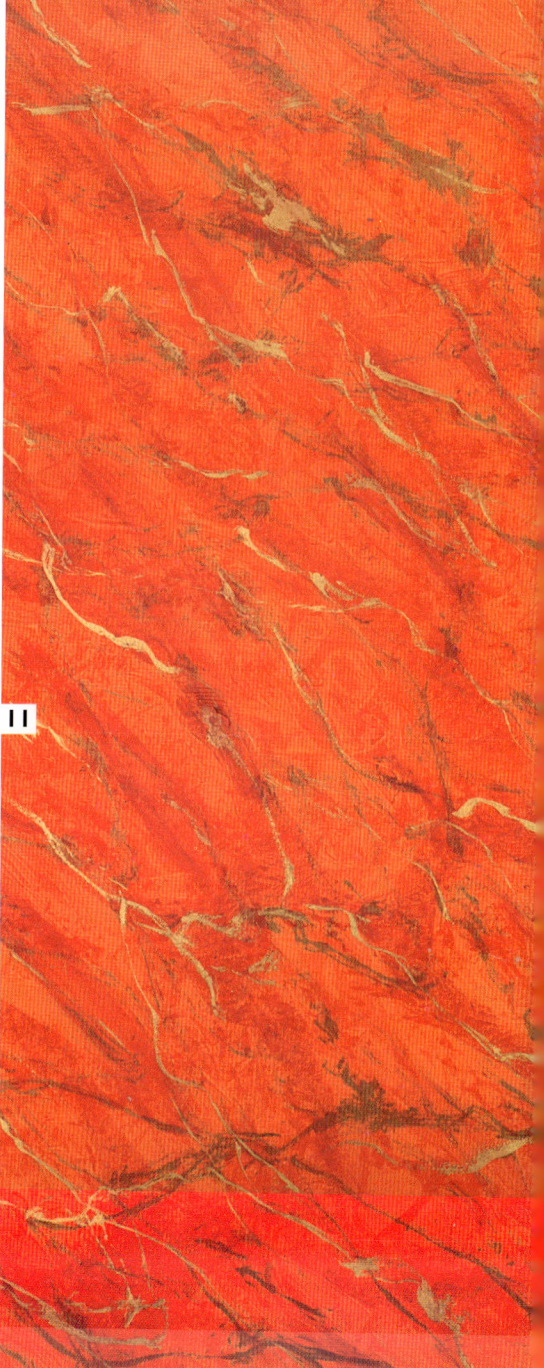

# BLUE MARBLE

## RECIPE

### BLUE MARBLE

**LEVEL OF EXPERTISE:**

**RECOMMENDED ON:** Panelling, floors, mouldings, columns, tabletops, bath surrounds, fireplace mantels, furnishings, accessories

**NUMBER OF PEOPLE:** 1

**TOOLS:** Newspaper or dust sheets; rubber gloves; paint trays; paint stirrers; paint roller for applying base coat; large-size household sponge; sea sponge; palette; paper for testing sponge marks; water for wetting and washing out sponges; silver leaf; gold size to adhere foil; feather to smooth glue; paint pad to apply varnish

**BASE COAT:** Powder-blue silk-finish emulsion paint

**APPLIED FINISH:** 4 silk-emulsion paint colours, plus silver leaf for veining

◆ Sail blue

◆ Caribbean green

◆ Dark teal

◆ Salmon

**VARNISH:** Use oil-based varnish

---

Colours from an Impressionist painting, just a hint of silver veining . . . this fantasy marble could easily liven up a room or give a worn old object new life.

And it's simple to do. That's because it relies mainly on one of the most easily mastered decorative painting techniques—sponging on, which involves "printing" multiple layers of sponged impressions over your base coat. It's these multiple layers that give the finish the sense of depth you get when you look at genuine marble.

You'll use two kinds of sponges to get extra variation in the impressions you make—household and sea sponge. The household sponge puts in a background pattern (over your base coat). Any size will do, but the larger sizes are easier to hold. Also, with the range of sponges available in most stores today, be sure to get the old-fashioned kind with small holes, not a "scrub-brush" type—the pattern will be too distinctive.

The sea sponge helps you add depth, by creating softer layers and blending your colours slightly. Because of the popularity of decorative painting, sea sponges are more readily available than ever. You can get them in craft and paint stores now, as well as in drug and chemist shops.

Because you're using emulsion paints, you can buy just one of each kind of sponge and wash them out between colours. Before you begin, however, you'll want to cut the edges off your sponges so that they have a more rounded, fishlike shape (more like the shapes you find in real marble).

Remember that a major distinctive feature of marble is its directional flow. In the previous recipe, for "Red Marble", you created fishlike shapes "swimming" *on the diagonal*. For this particular recipe, you want those same "fish" to swim *vertically*. Any imprints you put on your surface should be in the vertical direction.

BLUE MARBLE

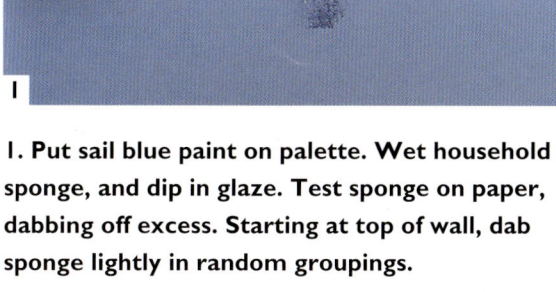

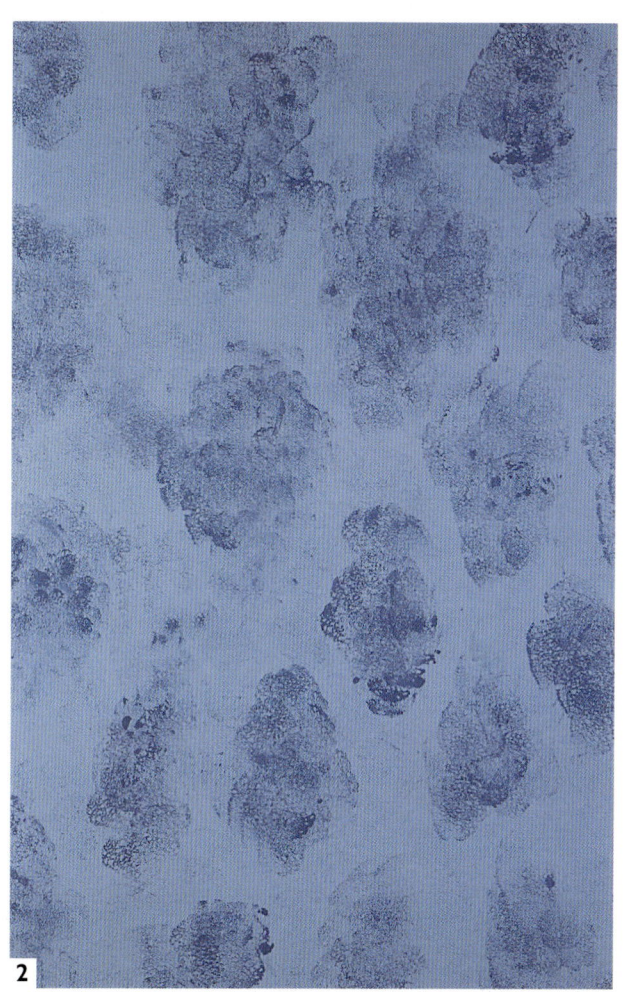

1. Put sail blue paint on palette. Wet household sponge, and dip in glaze. Test sponge on paper, dabbing off excess. Starting at top of wall, dab sponge lightly in random groupings.

2. Create "schools of fish" swimming in vertical direction. Overlap some "fish". Use only a little paint so that texture of sponge is visible.

### HOW TO GET THOSE SPARKLING SILVER VEINS

What really makes this marble sparkle is its silver veining. You can create it easily with commercially available products—silver leaf, which comes prepackaged in sheets, and gold size for fixing it in place, which comes in a small bottle. Both are usually available in specialist paint shops; be sure to follow the application and drying instructions for your particular brand. If you can't find them in your area, you can use silver paint. Apply it with a feather in the same manner as the gold paint in the previous recipe. The feather will also come in handy when applying the gold size. Use it to "feather out" the edges of the glue line you "draw on", giving your veining a more natural look.

THE RECIPES

## BLUE MARBLE

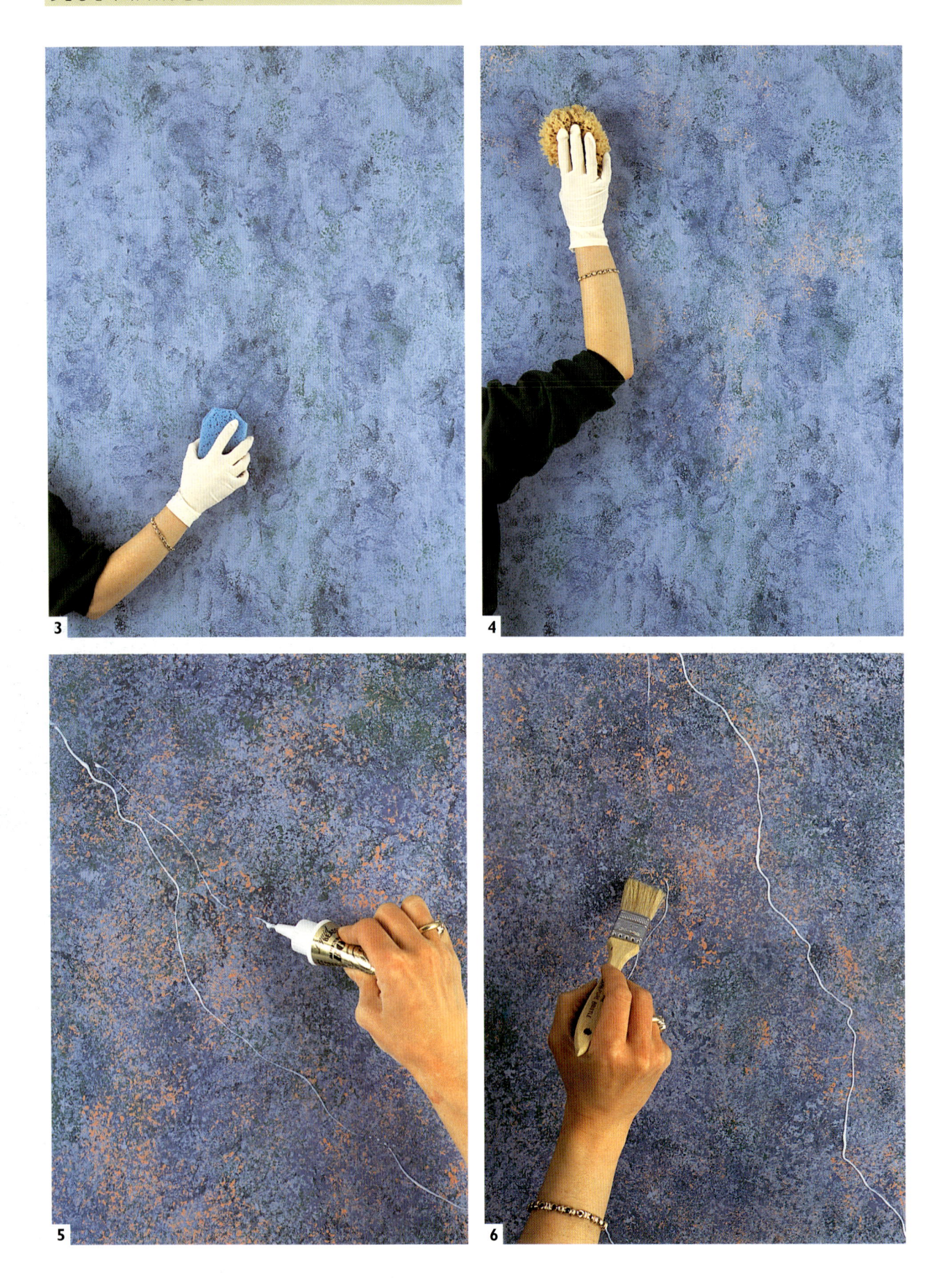

"FANTASY" MARBLING

# BLUE MARBLE

3. Repeat step 1 using Caribbean green paint and filling in between sail blue sponged impressions. Paint dries quickly, so you don't have to wait long before applying next layer. Repeat again, using dark teal paint. Overlap sail blue and Caribbean green impressions and fill in around edges.

4. Switch to sea sponge. Wet it first, then repeat Step 1, using salmon paint. Go over most of surface, blending colours and adding depth. Then with wet sea sponge, apply random impressions of three other paints (sail blue, Caribbean green, and dark teal). Rinse out sponge and let surface dry approximately ten minutes between each colour.

5. Let surface dry completely. Then, starting at top of wall, apply gold size in shape of veining. Squeeze out a thin layer, holding your wrist loosely so that you can make squiggly lines. (If you get gold size where you don't want it, wash it off immediately; it won't come off once dry.)

6. With feather or small, soft brush, "feather out" edges of gold size to create fade-away effect. Let glue dry, following manufacturer's recommendation, until it is opaque and tacky.

7. Press sheet of silver leaf over part of gold size, rub thumb over veining, and lift sheet off. (Silver leaf will remain on surface.) Repeat process until all size is covered with foil.

8. With paint pad, varnish surface in smooth, sweeping strokes. It is important to varnish this effect otherwise the silver leaf will tarnish. (See page 31 for varnishing tips.) Look of finished effect will vary, depending on light in which it is seen.

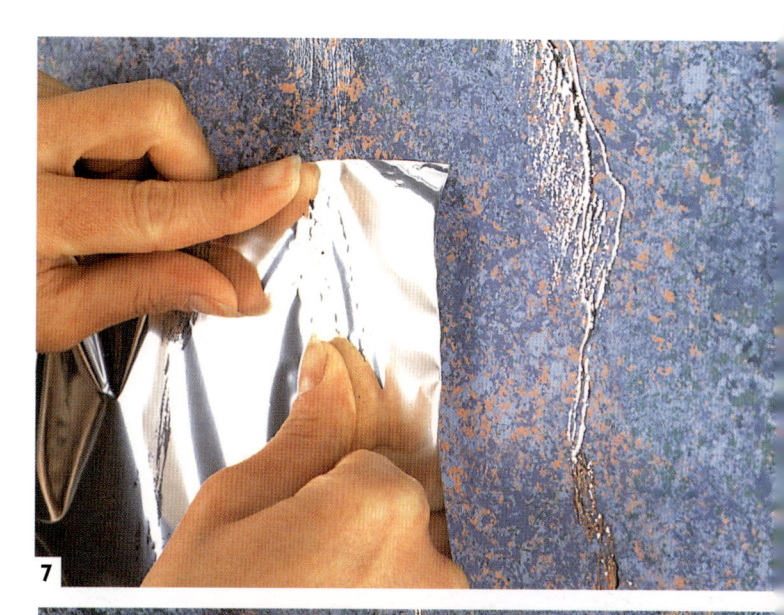

THE RECIPES

# SEDIMENTARY-STYLE MARBLE

## RECIPE
### SEDIMENTARY-STYLE MARBLE

**LEVEL OF EXPERTISE:**

**RECOMMENDED ON:** Walls, panelling, columns, tabletops, bath surrounds, furnishings, accessories

**NUMBER OF PEOPLE:** 2 recommended, depending on project size

**TOOLS:** Newspaper or dust sheets; face mask; rubber gloves; paint tray; paint roller for applying base coat; paint stirrers; plastic cups to hold paint; white spirit; 5cm household bristle brush; 2.5cm foam bristle brush; No. 5 sable brush; paper for testing tools on; 7.5 x 12cm cardboard pieces for "dragging" paint; paper towels; cotton rags for touch up; paint-scraping pad for splattering paint; paint pad to apply varnish

**BASE COAT:** Dove white silk-finish emulsion paint

**GLAZES:** Transparent oil glaze and 5 eggshell paint colours

- Saddle
- Turquoise
- Damson
- Clay
- Buff

**VARNISH:** Use oil-based varnish

---

If Santa Fe style inspires you, this finish may be just what you've been looking for. A great alternative to overstylized wallpaper patterns in this style, it evokes the type of stone you find at Uluru.

In the watercolourlike hues shown here, the finish is a real attention-getter. But, by using several shades of a neutral hue, you can easily "turn down" the colour intensity to "desert at daybreak". A beautiful tone-on-tone version could turn a room into the perfect showcase for a collection of Santa Fe furnishings, fabrics, and artefacts.

To do a whole room, you'll benefit from working with a partner. You'll need to paint in long strips across the room, and it will be helpful to have someone to move your ladder as you go. Or, you may find it easier to set up scaffolding so that you can move easily across your wall without having to walk up and down.

Practice is especially important with this finish. It is based on a traditional decorative painting technique used by wood grainers. Called "dragging", it can take a little time to master because it requires a somewhat steady hand. (You can find a detailed guide to dragging—as well as other dragged finishes you might like to try once you've mastered the technique—beginning on page 180 of the first edition of *Recipes for Surfaces*.) Dragging can be done with a wide range of tools—combs, paint brushes, even steel wool. For this finish, the paint is dragged with a piece of cardboard.

A small detail that will make a big difference with this technique: how you get your cardboard to the size you need. Don't cut it with scissors. Rip it, to get a feathered edge. But rip it neatly—you don't want any big gaps in the edge because too much paint might pass through them and distort the effect. Be sure you test your piece of cardboard before using it on your wall to make sure it creates a pleasing pattern.

"FANTASY" MARBLING

# SEDIMENTARY-STYLE MARBLE

**1.** With 2.5cm foam brush, paint on horizontal stripes of saddle glaze. Hold brush flat against wall, varying pressure as you go across surface to create dark and light spots. Lines should be wavy, even streaky. Be sure to leave some white space between lines.

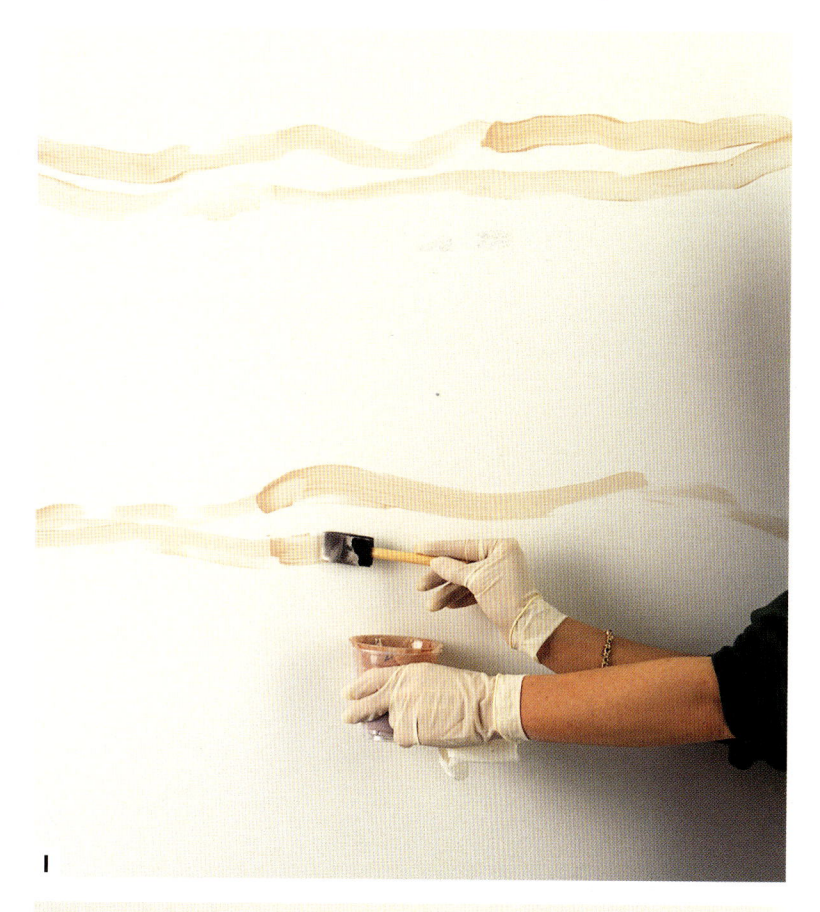

**2.** Immediately after you paint lines, "drag" over them with a 7.5 x 12cm piece of cardboard (that you have carefully ripped, not cut with scissors). Wiggle cardboard as you drag it across. Wipe cardboard on paper towel after each pass. Replace cardboard when it gets saturated. Let glaze dry.

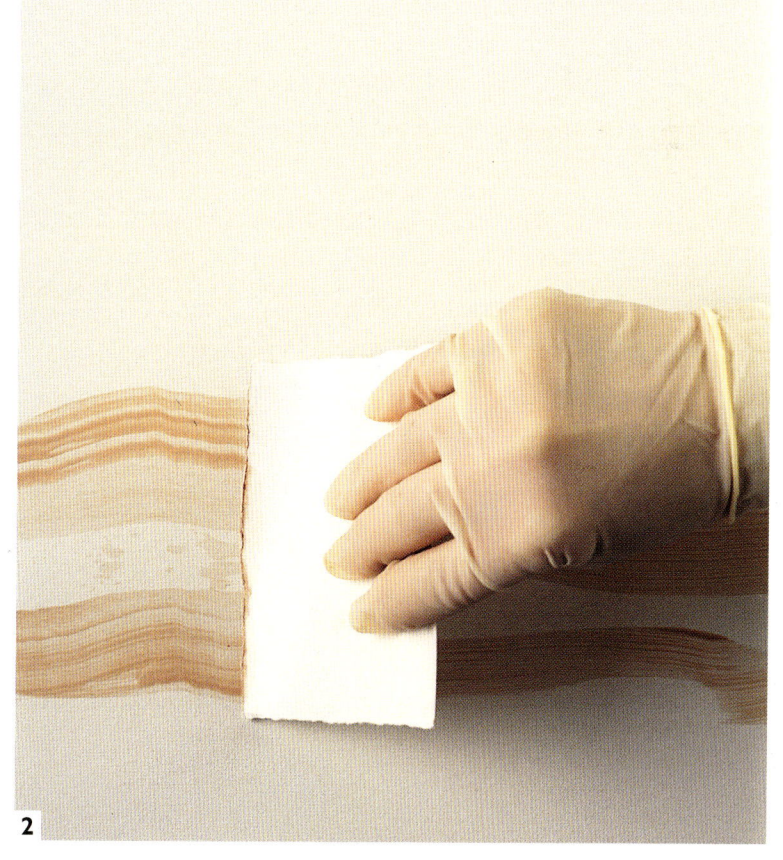

**THE RECIPES**

## SEDIMENTARY-STYLE MARBLE

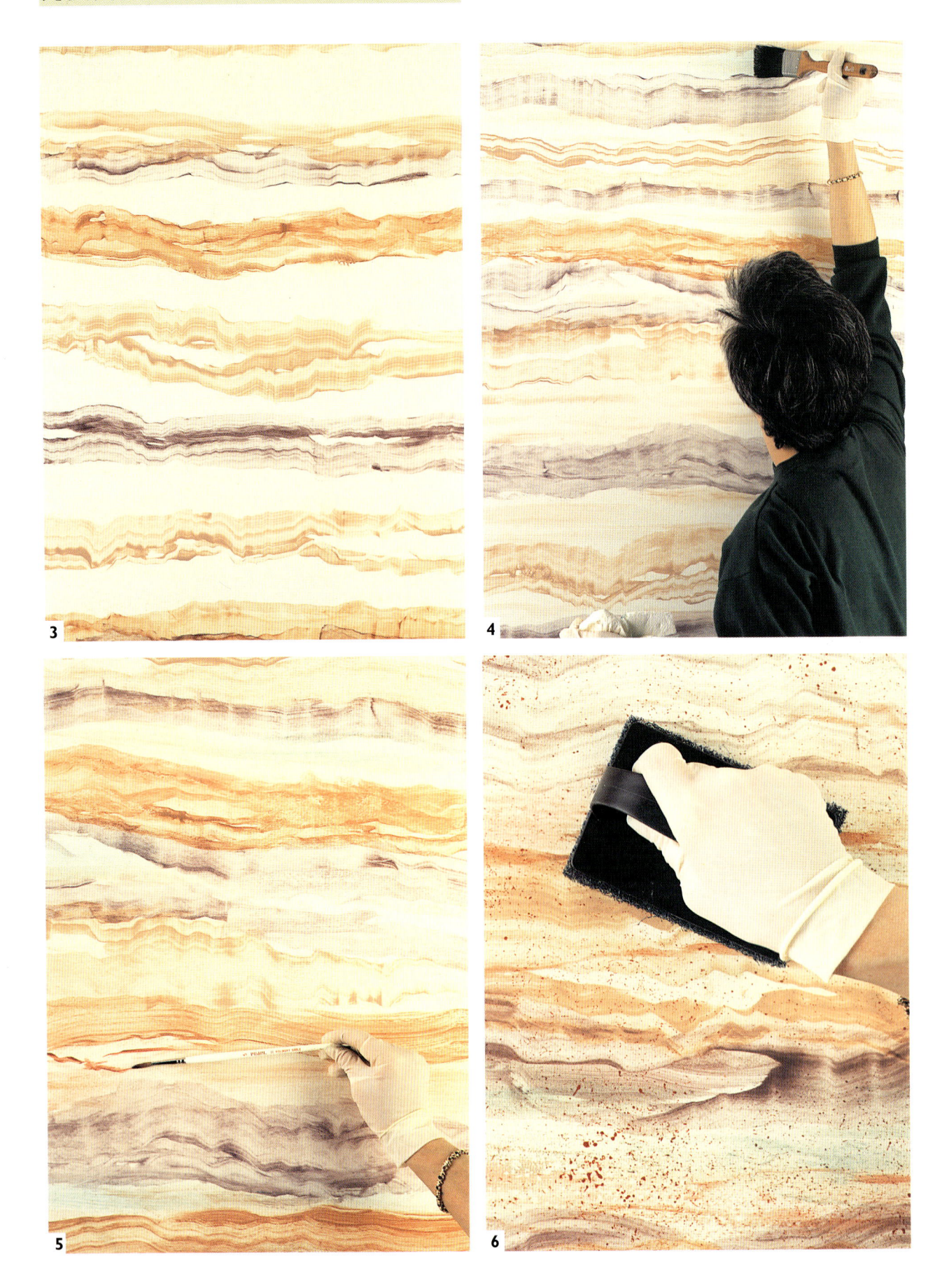

**3**

**4**

**5**

**6**

112  "FANTASY" MARBLING

# SEDIMENTARY-STYLE MARBLE

**3.** Repeat process with damson glaze, putting in damson stripes between saddle stripes. Let glaze dry.

**4.** Paint on water streaks of buff glaze, filling in between saddle and damson stripes. Drag over buff glaze with dry 5cm household bristle brush. Let glaze dry. Paint on turquoise glaze. Use it as an accent— paint in between every few stripes, over buff glaze in spots. If it gets too dark, wipe off with cotton rag.

**5.** With clay glaze and No. 5 sable brush, add in brush strokes to bring out some veining. Hold brush by tip, and roll it, to make wavy, wiggly lines. Don't hold brush like a pencil—the looser you hold it, the more natural lines will look. Add more veining with brush and turquoise glaze, then with buff glaze. The more lines and layers of colour you add, the more you get a feeling of depth.

**6.** Pour some damson glaze in paint tray. Dip in paint-scraping pad, and "off-load" excess glaze on paper. Dab pad randomly over surface. (Note: this is the "Spattering" technique. For a detailed guide, see page 148.) Fill in with spots in areas where surface is least busy.

**7.** With a paint pad, varnish surface for marblelike sheen. See page 95 for instructions.

7

**THE RECIPES**

# CHAPTER NINE

## REASONABLE REPLICAS

You could study for years to learn how to reproduce some of the materials featured in this chapter, or you can create these attractive, fun, and easily attainable versions by simply following the recipes found here—without all the studying.

With these finishes you have the opportunity to get a classic or "decorator" look at a fraction of the cost. The warmth and depth of frescoed walls can be yours without the plaster and painstaking execution, thanks to a technique as simple as polishing shoes. A country kitchen with a real brick floor may be a dream based on something you saw in a magazine, but you can capture some of the rusticity with the brick finish that is included in this chapter, using the easily mastered technique of sponging.

**Decorative painting lets you capture a late-afternoon cloudy sky, shown here embellished with grapevine motifs in a designer showhouse room.**

If you've always wanted fabric-covered walls, take a look at the recipe for "Moiré", reminiscent of a beautiful blue Chinese water silk. (The same simple graining technique lets you mimic wood panelling.) And what could be more classic, or more refreshing on a dark day, than a cloud ceiling—one that, instead of painting, you rub on with a cloth.

Before starting on any of these recipes, take some time to study the materials you plan to reproduce. There's no need to copy them exactly. What you're striving for is the general look and feel. For example, how do the natural creases in leather fall? How do clouds *really* look? It's when you can transfer the unique characteristics of a material to your painted finish that it really takes on life. To get you started, we've included photographs of the materials. But take your research further. That's what artists do, and it pays off.

Once you're ready to begin, a positive, can-do attitude will be your best friend. Don't be intimidated by how difficult you've *heard* it is to do a finish. The best way to gain confidence is to practise on some sample boards first.

FRESCO

| RECIPE |
| :---: |
| **FRESCO** |

**LEVEL OF EXPERTISE:**

**RECOMMENDED ON:**
Walls

**NUMBER OF PEOPLE:** 1

**TOOLS:** Newspapers or dust sheets; paint tray; paint stirrers; white spirit; face mask; rubber gloves; paint roller to apply base coat; cotton sheeting, cut into squares about 30cm

◇ **BASE COAT:** Linen white silk-finish emulsion paint

◆ **GLAZE:** Transparent oil glaze and pumpkin eggshell paint

**VARNISH:** Optional

---

Nancy and Jeffrey Brooks, the interior designers of the show-house room (shown *opposite*), assisted Nick Devlin, the muralist, by stencilling in individual leaf shapes for the background of the grapevine.

---

When it comes to giving a room the soft, warm glow you see in traditional old homes and the pages of magazines, few finishes do more than fresco. An ancient technique associated with mural painting and having its roots in Italy, fresco involves applying pigment to still-wet plaster.

Instead of struggling with plaster and trowel, however, you can get some of the same depth of colour and subtle textured look with paint. This is a great technique for beginners. There are no complicated brush strokes to learn—in fact, it's as simple as polishing furniture.

Using an easy motion, you make small circles all over your surface, then blend the edges of the circles into one another. Where the circles overlap, you get the lights and darks that give the finish great depth.

Two keys to this technique: use only a little glaze on your rag at a time, and make sure your rag is fluff-free and that the ends of the rag stay tucked in (gathered up into your palm) at all times.

You may be surprised at how dark you have to stain your glaze just to get the subtle colour you see here—and at how dark the glaze is when you first dab it on the wall. But it makes sense when you think of all the rubbing you'll do.

The best advice is, if you want your glaze to be the colour of the lightest chip in the row on a paint chart, stain it until it is the colour of the darkest chip in that row. Otherwise, you're sure to be disappointed because the more you rub the finish, the more paint you remove and, thus, the lighter it will be.

Because you're working with oil-based glaze, you'll have plenty of time to blend your circles well before the edges dry. But do keep in mind that this technique is a "one-off": once it's dry, it can't be changed. You need to step back from your work periodically to see the light-and-dark effects you're creating. And you must work in sections. If you have to stop, do it at an inconspicuous place: i.e., over a doorway or before starting the next wall.

**THE RECIPES**

# FRESCO

**1.** Fold your rag up into your hand so that all the ends are tucked in. Dab a little pumpkin glaze on your rag. Rub the glaze onto the wall with a circular motion. Then, working in sections about 1 x 1m, randomly select spots within the section you're working on, and rub on more circles.

**2.** Blend the edges of one circle into the next. Dip your rag into the glaze again, taking care to pick up just a little, and repeat process, section by section.

**3.** A close-up of the finished effect reveals its subtle texture and depth of colour.

**REASONABLE REPLICAS**

# LEATHER

## RECIPE
### LEATHER

**LEVEL OF EXPERTISE:**

**RECOMMENDED ON:** Walls

**NUMBER OF PEOPLE:** 2 recommended, but 1 can do

**TOOLS:** Newspapers or dust sheets; rags; rollers to apply base coat and glaze; paint trays; paint stirrers; white spirit; face mask; rubber gloves; scissors; plastic dry-cleaner bags or super-lightweight plastic sheeting (1mm), enough to cover your entire surface

◆ **BASE COAT:** Barn red silk-finish emulsion paint

◆ **GLAZE:** Transparent oil glaze and garnet oil-based eggshell paint

**VARNISH:** Optional

---

Leather is taking home furnishings by storm these days—but we're not talking about the "library look", with matching burgundy deep-buttoned chairs, or a midnight assault of Harley-Davidson black. Leather now often appears in concert with other fabrics and textures—for instance, a leather sofa sporting canvas cushions might be paired with denim-upholstered armchairs and leather scatter cushions.

Colourwise, you can hardly go wrong by sticking with the deep, rich hues of the "fine Corinthian leather" shown here; it can lend warmth to any setting. But consider that today you have a lot more freedom—and a lot more sources of inspiration. Real leather comes in more colours than ever, from the most traditional hunting green to shocking pink, baby blue, and royal purple. What might work in your rooms?

If the leather look is for you, you'll need to do a bit of advanced planning: start saving those bags your clothes come home from the dry cleaners in. In fact, if you plan to do a whole room, ask your family and friends to save theirs, too. You'll need enough bags to cover your entire surface because the bags get full of paint and are tricky to reuse.

Getting the leather look is easier than you think. You roll on glaze over your base coat, slap on the bags one next to the other, smooth them out to create the "crevices" you find in leather, then pull them off. Because you're using oil-based glaze—and covering it with plastic—you have plenty of time to get those "crevices" just the way you want them before the paint dries. And the bags won't fall off the walls as you work; they stick to the paint until you're ready to take them down. The technique is more easily done by two—it's helpful to have someone assist you in putting up the plastic. But one person can definitely do it on his or her own, as you see here.

Note that with the leather finish, you want the "crevices" to run in many directions, just as they do on the real thing. (For a similar, but more "directional" look, see "Plastic-Wrap Ragging Off".) This is what gives the finish its character. To get this, you can just smooth out the bags and let them go however they go, or you can step back and decide how to arrange them to your liking.

Before you begin, mask off everything in the room you don't want to get glaze on (i.e., ceiling, door frames, windows). Then, turn dry-cleaner bags into painting tools: with scissors, cut the edges off the bags, and open the sides.

**THE RECIPES**

## LEATHER

1. Over dry base coat, apply glaze with roller. Then immediately begin putting bags over wet glaze, working with a partner, if possible, to make the process easier. Do one entire wall at a time. Be sure you have enough plastic to cover entire surface.

2. Smooth bags, forming "creases" that create the leather look.

3. Once "smoothing" is complete, pull all bags off at once.

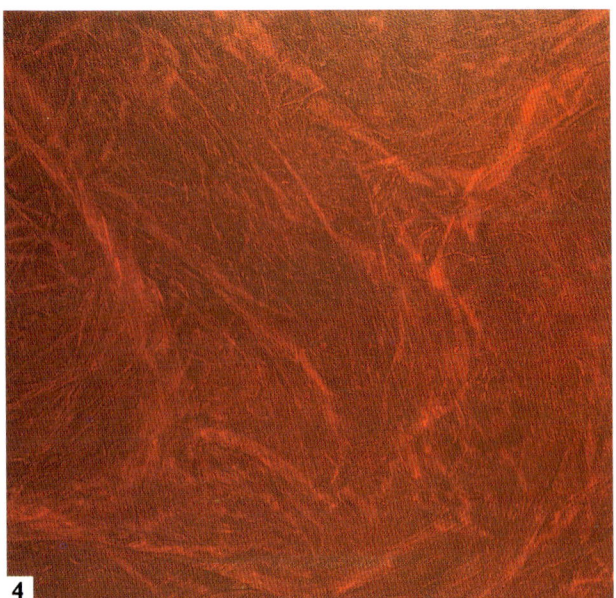

4. A view of the leather look finish shows the creases across the surface in many directions.

# STUCCO

Here is an increasingly popular colour combination you might not have considered before—maize and ash. The maize brightens a room, while the ash keeps it well within the range of easy-to-live-with neutrals.

In this recipe, combining yellows and greys also gives you an appealing approximation of stucco. And you can take it a step further: pair the finish with the "Stone-work" effect on page 90 for a pleasing rendition of an old stone wall. The stucco is the background, while the stones fill in here and there, as if the stucco has crumbled and chipped away in spots.

You'll be pleased at how easy it is to master the technique that gives you this sophisticated effect. Sponging on—in which you use a sea sponge to apply glazes to your surface—gives you the subtle texture of stucco.

You can find sea sponges in paint, craft, and DIY stores, as well as chemists and cosmetic shops these days. Work with a piece of sponge cut to the size of your hand so that it's comfortable for you. (For more tips on sponging, read the recipes for "Marbling". For a detailed guide to sponging refer to the first edition of *Recipes for Surfaces*, Chapter Five.)

The colours in stucco are the same as those in the recipe for "Stone"; but here they are softened by the addition of white. The glazes are made of emulsion paint, watered down to a watercolourlike quality. (The mix that gives you this subtle wash of colour is about 20 per cent paint, 80 per cent water.)

Be sure to mix enough of each glaze for the entire project so that your colours are consistent throughout. Another colour-consistency tip: stir glazes often as you work. When you first dip your sponge into a glaze, you pick up more water than paint and, over time, the paint settles to the bottom. You may need to add a bit more water as you go through your projects.

The key to this technique is working layer by layer. You always need to be aware of how much paint is on your sponge. This is a building-up process—and it can happen much quicker than you think. It's easy to get too much paint on your surface. You don't want the finish to be too bright. You want a soft, natural look—a cloudy finish with a lot of depth. This is where your "designer's eye" comes in and where it's advantageous to work in thin layers: you get more time to see how the finish is building up. Have patience—you can always add more paint, but once you get a dark spot, you're in trouble because your eye will aways go to that spot. You might end up having to balance the spot with another or make the whole room darker.

---

### RECIPE
**STUCCO**

**LEVEL OF EXPERTISE:**

**RECOMMENDED ON:** Walls, ceilings

**NUMBER OF PEOPLE:** 1

**TOOLS:** Newspapers or dust sheets; paint tray; paint stirrers; roller to apply base coat; face mask; rubber gloves; sea sponge; paper for testing sponge

◆ **BASE COAT:** Dove white matt emulsion paint

**GLAZES:** Watered-down emulsion paint (20 per cent paint, 80 per cent water)

◆ Light maize

◆ Light ash

**VARNISH:** No (sheen would detract from look)

---

THE RECIPES 121

## STUCCO

Well-worn and weathered stucco features an appealing mix of soft, almost neutral hues.

1

2

122   REASONABLE REPLICAS

## STUCCO

1. Pour light maize paint into tray. Wet sponge with water. Mix paint and water in paint tray to a very watery consistency. Keep a rag handy in case you have to clean up any drips. Dip sponge into paint and water mixture and wring out. Blot on newspaper to remove excess paint and to check the impression being made by the sponge.

2. Bunch sponge up in your hand, holding it straight. Pat sponge lightly to surface, working in a 1.2m section. Vary the direction of the sponge by shifting your wrist when the sponge is in the air. Move your pats to concentrate in different areas and fill in between the heaviest spots as the paint diminishes on the sponge. Work until the sponge is almost dry. Before you repeat the sponging, step back and examine the distribution of the paint on the surface to see if the light and dark marks are pleasingly balanced.

3. Re-dip sponge in glaze and unload most of the colour before you repeat step 2. Always test your sponge before applying it to the wall, to make sure you have the colour you want. Step back from your project as you work to make sure you're "making waves", that is, creating lighter and darker patches of colour. Repeat the process with light ash colour. Starting with light impressions and building up colour intensity through layering.

4. A close-up of this delicate finish discloses the pleasing mix of light maize and light ash that "says" stucco.

THE RECIPES

## CLOUDY SKY

### RECIPE

**CLOUDY SKY**

**LEVEL OF EXPERTISE:**

**RECOMMENDED ON:** Ceilings

**NUMBER OF PEOPLE:** 1

**TOOLS:** Newspaper or dust sheets; face mask; rubber gloves; paint tray; paint roller for applying base coat; white spirit; paint stirrers; 30cm square cotton rags

**BASE COAT:** Sky blue matt emulsion paint

**APPLIED FINISH:** White oil-based enamel paint

**VARNISH:** No

What better way to transform a small room than by opening it to the outdoors? If breaking through the walls or the roof just aren't options, you can use this recipe to bring the "wild blue yonder" inside.

Before you begin, spend some time looking up. Study the sky under a variety of weather conditions and times of day, and sketch or photograph cloud patterns you like.

Keep in mind, however, that puffy clouds can be tougher to paint than wispy ones. The wispy clouds created with this recipe are easier to master and still give a satisfying effect.

The most likely place you'll want to execute this finish is on the ceiling; so give some thought now to how you'll paint up there. Artists usually try to set up a moveable, wheeled platform called an access tower, which you can either rent or build yourself. The tower should be high enough to bring you within comfortable arm's reach of the ceiling either when you're lying on your back or kneeling, whichever way you're more comfortable painting.

This recipe employs three ways of using a cotton rag: dragging, pulling, and ragging on with it. Working with a rag instead of a brush will probably be a blessing for the beginning painter. You're less likely to end up with a stereotypical notion of what clouds should look like with this less-traditional painting tool. Be sure to prepare your rags carefully before you start. They need to be fluff free so that you don't end up with any foreign particles in your painted finish. Cut your cloth with scissors or pinking shears to prevent fraying; you may want to machine wash and dry it, then run a lint roller or masking tape over it to remove fuzz.

You'll find additional instructions for the ragging-on technique under "Corduroy Ragging On". (For a detailed guide to ragging, see the first edition of *Recipes for Surfaces*, page 110.)

# CLOUDY SKY

**1.** Fold rag to form long, flat "printing surface". Dip rag into paint, then blot off on paper until almost dry. Working in sections, apply with soft, curved, sweeping strokes.

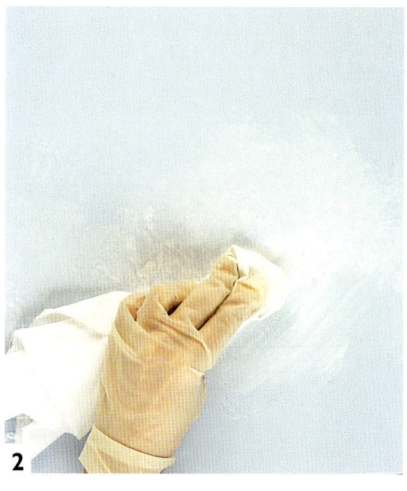

**2.** While paint is still wet, pull rag through sweeps of white paint to create hazy effect.

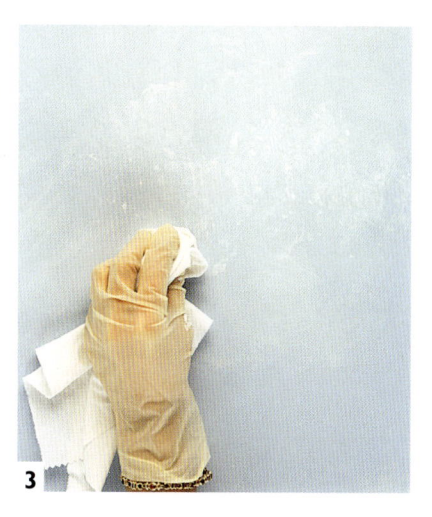

**3.** Crumple rag in hand, and dip in paint. Off-load excess until rag is almost dry. "Rag on" over surface to further soften effect and enhance airy, cloudlike feel. Touch rag to surface lightly, turning wrist when rag is in air to vary impressions. Dab wall in spots randomly so that impressions made when rag has most paint on it are scattered throughout.

**4.** Cloudy sky at 10 a.m. Or, change the colours and get a late-afternoon look, as in the photo of the designer showhouse room, page 116.

THE RECIPES

# BRICK

## RECIPE

### BRICK

**LEVEL OF EXPERTISE:**

**RECOMMENDED ON:** Walls, floors

**NOT RECOMMENDED ON:** Highly carved surfaces, small objects

**NUMBER OF PEOPLE:** 1

**TOOLS:** Newspaper or dust sheets; face mask; rubber gloves; paint trays; paint roller; white spirit; piece of cardboard, about 10 x 12cm; craft knife; a brick (optional — to trace size of and examine colours of); low-tack masking tape; plastic spoon to press down tape lines; foam brush (geared to size of job); sea sponge; paper for testing sponge imprint; varnishing pad

**BASE COAT:** Silk-finish emulsion paint—2 paint colours: paint on first colour, mortar, let dry, then tape over to mask out mortar, and apply second colour, melon

◆ Mortar

◆ Melon

**APPLIED FINISH:** 3 oil-based eggshell paint colours

◆ Terra cotta

◆ Brown

◆ Black

**VARNISH:** Required for floors

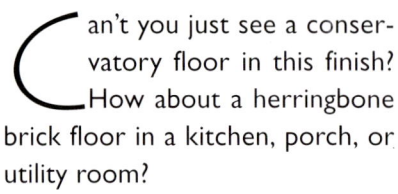

Can't you just see a conservatory floor in this finish? How about a herringbone brick floor in a kitchen, porch, or utility room?

The simple decorative-painting techniques of "sponging on" give you the ruddy-red bricks, while the colour in between is simply a mortar base coat, kept glaze-free during the sponging process with masking tape.

For wood floors in poor condition, paint can be an ideal remedy. You need to prepare them properly, by repairing, stripping, sanding, and priming them, as needed. (For a guide to surface preparation, see Chapter Three.)

Floor paint is most likely your best choice for the base coat, topped by oil-based glazes. You'll also want to apply several coats of varnish made for flooring to protect your design. Try to get varnish with a matt finish; too much shine on the surface might spoil the effect.

Keep in mind, too, that with floors you must plan to "paint yourself out of the room". You'll end up starting over if you walk over your finish before it dries.

In creating a herringbone pattern, you apply tape lines on a diagonal to form an angled grid. The space between lines should be the width of one brick. The best way to set the width is to trace an actual brick on cardboard twice, cut out the two shapes, and use them to mark the space between lines. You also need to determine the pitch of your diagonal lines and the angle their intersections should form.

BRICK

1. Cut out two cardboard rectangles the size of bricks. (To get size right, trace actual brick.) Put up diagonal tape guidelines in one direction across surface. Lines should be width of one brick apart; use cardboard-cut-out bricks to measure off spaces.

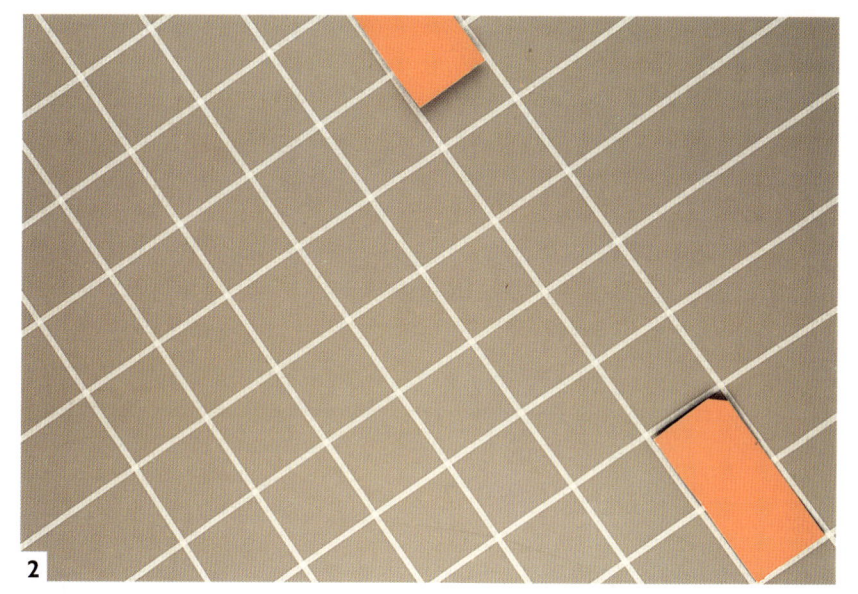

2. Apply tape guidelines on diagonal in opposite direction—again, width of one brick apart—so tape forms angled grid on surface.

Find a few examples of brick herringbone, actual or in photos, including the one on the previous page; take your cue from them.

One challenge with this recipe: cutting out the correct pieces of tape from your initial grid to form the herringbone pattern. This can be tricky, so go slow. Stop often to check you're removing the right sections. If you make a mistake, just replace the tape and press it firmly back in place.

If classic red is too overpowering for your scheme, light pink, pale yellow, soft beige, white, or even a "fantasy" colour can work. But if you feel the effect of a whole wall would be too heavy-looking for your interior, consider interspersing a few bricks over a neutral background instead—as if the bricks were just visible where the plaster of an old wall had chipped away.

To begin this technique, apply mortar base coat with roller. Let dry overnight.

THE RECIPES

BRICK

**3.** Press all tape lines firmly in place with back of a spoon or a credit card to prevent seepage. With craft knife, starting in one corner of surface, cut out parts of tape lines to form herringbone pattern. This can be tricky, so go slow. Stop often to make sure you're removing right part of tape lines. If you make a mistake, just replace tape and press firmly back in place.

**4.** Using foam brush, paint over entire surface with melon paint in uneven, criss-crossing strokes to begin creating "rough" brick surface. Let dry.

**5.** Dip sea sponge into white spirit and wring well. Pour terra cotta glaze colour into paint tray. Dab sponge into paint, then blot off and test impression on paper. "Sponge on" over entire surface: repeatedly touch sponge lightly to wall, twisting your wrist or arm when sponge is off surface to vary impression. After dipping sponge in terra cotta, don't make marks all in one small area or you'll get a dark spot; touch surface randomly to distribute evenly when sponge has most glaze on it.

**6.** Repeat step 5 with black glaze.

**7.** Repeat step 5 with brown glaze. Apply black more sparingly, however, so that finish doesn't get too dark.

**8.** Remove tape guidelines. Varnish surface, following instructions on page 95.

**9.** The finished product.

REASONABLE REPLICAS

BRICK

THE RECIPES 129

# MOIRÉ

## RECIPE

### MOIRÉ

**LEVEL OF EXPERTISE:**

**RECOMMENDED ON:** Flat, even surfaces—walls, including below chair rail as faux wainscotting, tabletops, furniture

**NOT RECOMMENDED ON:** Highly carved surfaces, small objects

**NUMBER OF PEOPLE:** 2 recommended, especially for large jobs requiring a ladder

**TOOLS:** Newspaper or dust sheets; face mask; rubber gloves; paint roller for applying base coat; paint tray; paint stirrers; 5cm low-tack masking tape; chalk pencil; spirit level; foam paint brush; paint container; no. 10 heart graining tool; graining comb; cheesecloth, cut into small squares

**BASE COAT:** Light blue matt emulsion paint

**GLAZE:** Transparent oil glaze and oil-based eggshell paint

**VARNISH:** Optional

---

Just the mention of "graining" may be enough to make those familiar with decorative painting hesitate. Certainly, realistically reproducing wood grains might take years of practise, but there is plenty of room in between for creating attractive effects with the same tools.

That being said, however, keep in mind that practise and a steady, experienced hand will still be your best help with this recipe.

The tools you use to create the look of that satiny, watermarked fabric called moiré are the same as the wood grainer's: a heart grainer (no. 10 size) and a graining comb. The tools are available in paint and art supply stores. The combs come in a package with several sizes. For your project, choose a comb that makes an imprint similar to the pattern your graining tool makes; similar width of the tools' "teeth" is what you should be looking at in making your choice. If you can't find a comb that's similar, all isn't lost; the difference will just make the strips stand out more from one another than you see here.

Another way to get an overall similarity to your finish is to count as you work. This method of monitoring your work without agonizing over it can be used with many of the techniques. In this case, it means that when you start graining over a strip of wet glaze, you count the number of squiggles you make and then generally repeat that same number in subsequent strips. You don't want each row to be the same, but if you look at rows of wood panelling, you can see there is a relationship between the proportion of the grains from one panel to another. That's the kind of similarity you want.

Note that the shorter the distance you do your graining over, the easier the technique will be for you. A great place to do it is below a chair rail in place of wainscotting.

If you are doing it over a whole wall, you'll need a partner—one person to apply the glaze, and another to do the graining before the glaze dries. Don't switch jobs midway through the project. The way each person does decorative painting is as personal as his or her signature—a switch to a lighter touch or a wavier graining line will stand out and distract from the overall effect.

Note, too, that for a whole wall, you'll be working with a ladder, which can be tricky to get on and off of while keeping your hand steady. You'll need that second person to move the ladder for you and vice versa.

Whatever happens, don't lift your graining tool off the wall in mid-strip. The spot where you stopped will be extremely noticeable. If you must stop, you'll need to repaint the strip and start graining again.

MOIRÉ

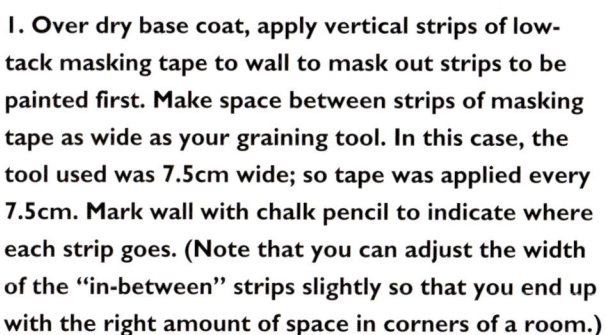

1. **Over dry base coat, apply vertical strips of low-tack masking tape to wall to mask out strips to be painted first. Make space between strips of masking tape as wide as your graining tool. In this case, the tool used was 7.5cm wide; so tape was applied every 7.5cm. Mark wall with chalk pencil to indicate where each strip goes. (Note that you can adjust the width of the "in-between" strips slightly so that you end up with the right amount of space in corners of a room.)**

2. **As you move across your surface, use a spirit level to check that strips are straight.**

THE RECIPES

# MOIRÉ

**3.** With foam brush or small roller, paint glaze over first untaped strip of wall. Start at bottom and stroke on glaze from side to side.

**5.** Wrap piece of cheesecloth on end of your finger and dab out any drips. Then move on to rest of wall, repeating steps 3, 4, and 5. Wipe graining tool off on cloth between passes. When all the untaped strips have been painted, take down tape and let dry overnight.

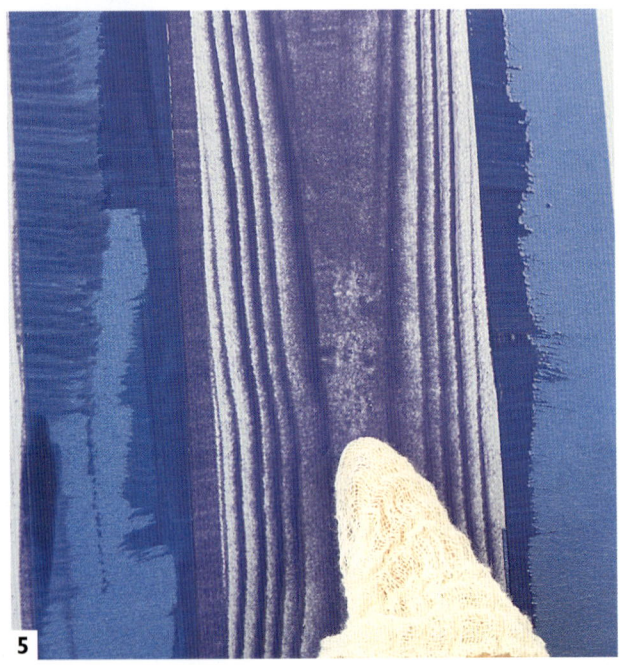

**4.** Immediately after painting strip, while glaze is still wet, go over strip with graining tool, starting at top of strip and rocking tool from side to side to get effect. Let tape be your guide as you rock tool. Do not lift tool off wall while moving down strip. (If you do, you'll need to repaint strip and start over.)

**6.** With foam brush, apply glaze to first of remaining strips to be painted, running brush down strip in short vertical strokes.

132   REASONABLE REPLICAS

MOIRÉ

**7.** While glaze is still wet, go over strip with graining comb. Wiggle tool as you move down wall to get wavy lines. Keep strip as neat as possible, wiping off excess glaze that gets on adjacent painted surfaces with a rag.

**8.** The rich colours of the finish capture the feel of moiré, a tone-on-tone fabric. Tone-on-tone offers another benefit: it helps keep irregularities caused by a less-than-steady hand from standing out.

THE RECIPES   133

# CHAPTER TEN

## "TEXTURED" WALL FINISHES

What you do with the walls sets the stage for the look and feel of your rooms. In interior design today, "textures" are in fashion. You can't pick up a home-design magazine that doesn't show rooms mixing and matching them with ease. "Textured" wall finishes like the ones in this chapter offer simple and affordable ways to introduce the look into your interiors. The finishes are great complements to some of the newest decorating styles. Known as "global" or "ethnic" design, these styles incorporate natural and precious materials and crafts from Africa, Asia, South America, and the Middle East.

If you have just moved into your first home and have little in the way of furnishings, these textured finishes can be a blessing.

**The "textured" finish in this blue room gives an airy look to an otherwise small space.**

They can dress up and even become the focal point of small, boxy rooms, the eye-catching element guests "ooh and aah" over when they first walk in. The finishes can introduce a sense of quality and originality without sending you over budget.

They can also hold great appeal for the minimalist—whether you're one by choice or have become one out of necessity (as parents of small children often do). If loading a room with lots of (breakable) accessories and (tempting-to-tug-at) window treatments is out of the question, effects like the "Feather-Duster Finish" or "Corduroy Ragging On," are ways to inject some life without the fuss.

And they couldn't be more in keeping with today's trend toward relaxed design. Their natural exuberance allows them to hide a multitude of imperfections on walls in poor shape and makes them well suited to spaces that get much use and must serve multiple purposes. And, because you have painted walls, when your tastes change or you move into another life stage, you can alter them more easily than if you have wallpaper or fabric on the walls.

You'll note that the word "textured" appears in quotes here. That's because all the finishes are, of course, flat. The sense of texture comes from the tools and methods with which you apply the glaze to your walls. The finishes in this chapter employ traditional methods of decorative painting, but are often executed with rather nontraditional tools, from a paint scraper to plastic wrap. Let this inspire you to try some unconventional tools of your own.

The ragging techniques, traditionally done with cotton cloth or cheesecloth, are particularly open to suggestion. You'll see them using corduroy and plastics here. You can also try paper, lace netting, carpet underlay, thin canvas, sisal, or sacking (as long as they don't fray too much).

With all the recipes in this chapter (and in the book), you really need to test your paint colours and tool impressions on paper repeatedly before starting on the walls—especially if you are working with an experimental tool, it may take a while to get the effect you want.

Although these finishes were designed for walls, they can also suit other surfaces, including floors, ceilings, cabinetry, furniture, and accessories. Just be sure to check with your local paint shop to get the right paint for your project.

"TEXTURED" WALL FINISHES

FEATHER-DUSTER FINISH

## RECIPE

### FEATHER-DUSTER FINISH

**LEVEL OF EXPERTISE:**

**RECOMMENDED ON:** Walls, panelling

**NOT RECOMMENDED ON:** Highly carved surfaces, small surfaces

**NUMBER OF PEOPLE:** 1

**TOOLS:** Newspapers or dust sheets; paint tray; paint stirrers; roller to apply base coat; paper for testing imprints; face mask; rubber gloves; rags for touch up and clean up; feather duster

♦ **BASE COAT:** Coral silk-finish emulsion paint

♦ **APPLIED FINISH:** Salmon silk-finish emulsion paint

**GLAZE:** Optional

---

One reason we start this chapter with this finish is to get a point across: loosen up. You *can* get great effects quickly and easily. You *can* have fun *and* be creative. In decorative painting, anything can serve as a painting tool. Use your imagination, and you may well be pleasantly surprised at what you come up with.

That's exactly what happened here. In Nancy's continuing quest for lively, eye-catching finishes, she took a chance on a feather duster and came up with what can easily be a fast, affordable, and original alternative to wallcovering. Depending on the colours you choose, these feathery impressions can bring to mind anything from a tropical paradise (are those abstract palm trees?) to the retro look of flocked wallpaper. For the feather-duster look, you need to apply only a little paint, hold your tool perpendicular to your surface, and use a light touch. Be sure to practise first on paper.

Also, be sure to make sample boards in the colours you select for your base coat and glaze. As you can see here, this lively finish truly benefits from well-chosen colour choices.

1. Pour salmon glaze into paint tray. Hold feather duster perpendicular to paint tray, and dip bottom of feathers into glaze. Make several impressions on paper to test that you have proper amount of paint. Then, working in 90cm sections, touch feather duster lightly to wall, making imprints several centimeters apart until you cover entire section.

**THE RECIPES**

# FEATHER-DUSTER FINISH

**2. Re-dip feather duster in glaze, and make additional imprints in between those on surface. Continue filling in with imprints until you have overall pattern. Stand back from surface, as needed, to see where you need to fill in.**

**3. The all-over patterned effect can make a lively substitute for wallpaper.**

With any tool that makes a distinct impression (as compared to the muted imprints of a cotton rag), a strong contrast between base-coat and glaze colours can prove overwhelming. Colours from the same family will give you a much softer, effect without relinquishing the "texture".

One last word of advice: every feather duster is different, so you won't get the exact pattern you see here. Be sure to choose your feather duster with care. As in many decorative painting techniques, you're printing with your tool, and the imprint you get can make or break your finish.

If the duster's feathers are too long, they might droop and give a blurrier effect. This is neither good nor bad—it just means you should test extensively to make sure you're happy with the impression you get. If the impression doesn't suit you, you might try trimming the feathers before you go out and buy another feather duster. Your sample boards are good places to try out your feather-duster tools.

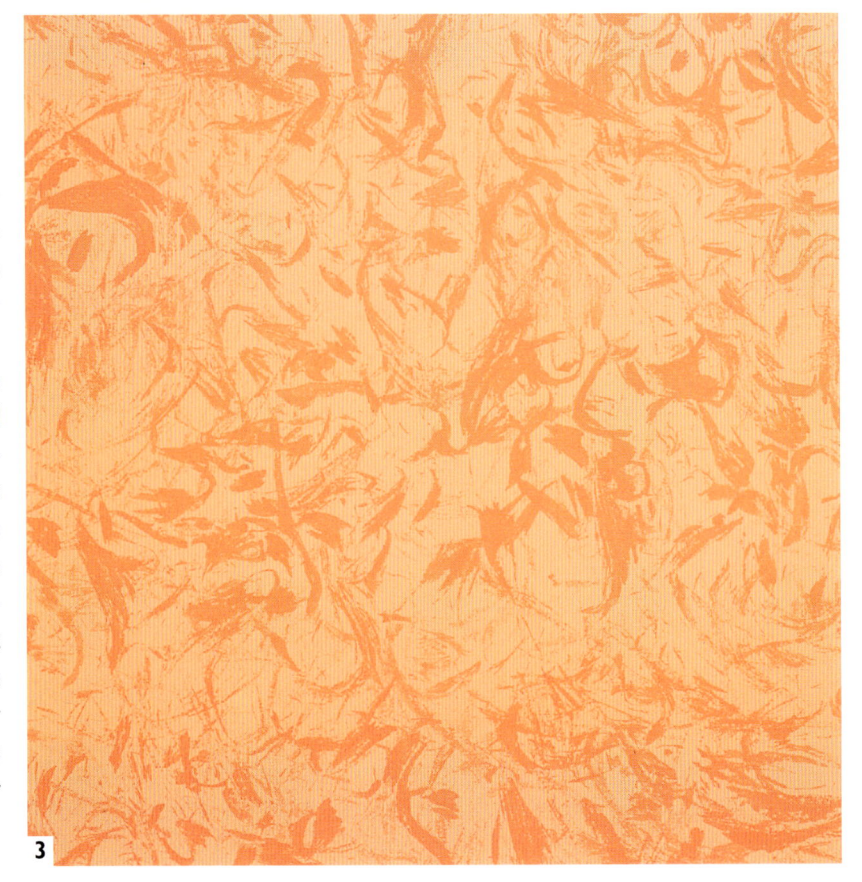

"Textured" WALL FINISHES

# CORDUROY RAGGING ON

## RECIPE
### CORDUROY RAGGING ON

**LEVEL OF EXPERTISE:**

**RECOMMENDED ON:** Walls, panelling, cabinetry, furniture, accessories

**NOT RECOMMENDED ON:** Highly carved surfaces

**NUMBER OF PEOPLE:** 1 or 2, depending on project size

**TOOLS:** Newspapers or dust sheets; paint tray; paint stirrers; roller to apply base coat; palette; paper for testing glaze; white spirit; face mask; rubber gloves; rags for touch up and clean up; corduroy, cut into 30cm squares; pinking shears and masking tape or lint roller to prepare corduroy

**BASE COAT:** Plum silk-finish emulsion paint

**GLAZE:** Transparent oil glaze and rose artists' oil paint

**VARNISH:** Optional

---

"Ragging", or cloth distressing, is one of the most popular decorative painting techniques. It is an easy one to master, and once you get comfortable with it, is especially rewarding because you can create so many different looks, depending on the material with which you "rag".

The distinctive finish you see here is a case in point. It's an example of ragging "on"—the additive version of ragging in which you apply glaze over your base coat with a piece of corduroy.

Even within this one technique, you can get different effects, depending on the kind of corduroy you use. Narrow ribs will give you a different pattern from wide ribs. In most cases, the wider the rib, the better. And don't use very fine corduroy; it's too thin to give you enough pattern.

For something a little different, try a light glaze over a darker base coat, as you see pictured on the following page. But keep in mind that the closer in colour base coat and glaze are, the more subtle the effect. This particularly comes into play if you're using wide rib corduroy, which gives you a strong pattern. Contrasting colours may make the finish too intense.

Note that when you're working with cloth you need to be extra careful of those foreign particles getting into your finish. Cloth will fray if you don't prepare it carefully. To ready your corduroy, cut it into 30cm squares, "pinking" the edges with a pinking shears to limit fraying. Next, wash and dry the cloths, then use masking tape or run a lint roller over them to remove as much "fluff" as possible.

How you hold the cloth is key. You want a flat surface to "print" with; so bunch the cloth in your hand, gathering the ends into your palm.

For best results, every time you dip your cloth into the glaze, test it. Use a paper plate or white paper for testing—not newsprint, which could get into the paint.

Be sure to use paint sparingly, and pat the cloth lightly against the wall so that the imprint of the fabric remains visible. After dabbing your cloth in the paint, touch it to the wall randomly—this way, the imprints made when the cloth has the most paint on it will be spread over your surface and not concentrated in one spot. Then go back and fill in, continuing until the cloth is almost dry. This is how you get the colour variations that add to the finish's distinctive look.

Composition is especially important with this finish. When you apply the glaze, don't limit yourself and work in one tiny area. Keep moving and reaching, up and down, side to side and keep stepping back to see your progress. Distribute the paint well when your cloth is at the same saturation level.

**THE RECIPES**

## CORDUROY RAGGING ON

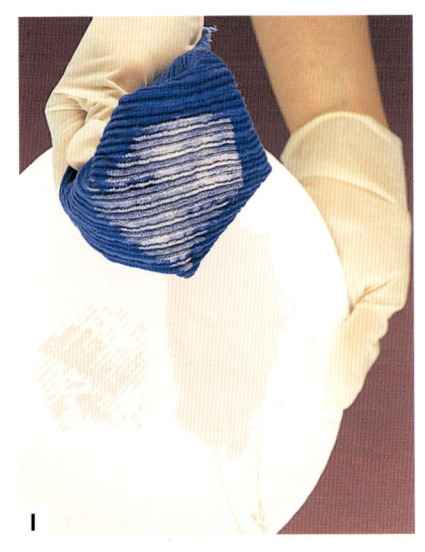

**1.** Bunch cloth in your hand to create flat, cushionlike surface, with all ends of rag tucked in. Dip cloth lightly into glaze and test on paper.

**2.** Press cloth lightly against wall so that imprint from cloth is clearly visible.

**3.** When you apply glaze, lift the rag and turn wrist so that all your impressions aren't going in same direction. Use glaze sparingly. Touch cloth to wall randomly so that imprints of same colour intensity will be spread over surface. Then fill in, continuing until cloth is almost dry. Dip cloth in glaze, test on paper plate, and repeat process on wall. Step back frequently to examine your work.

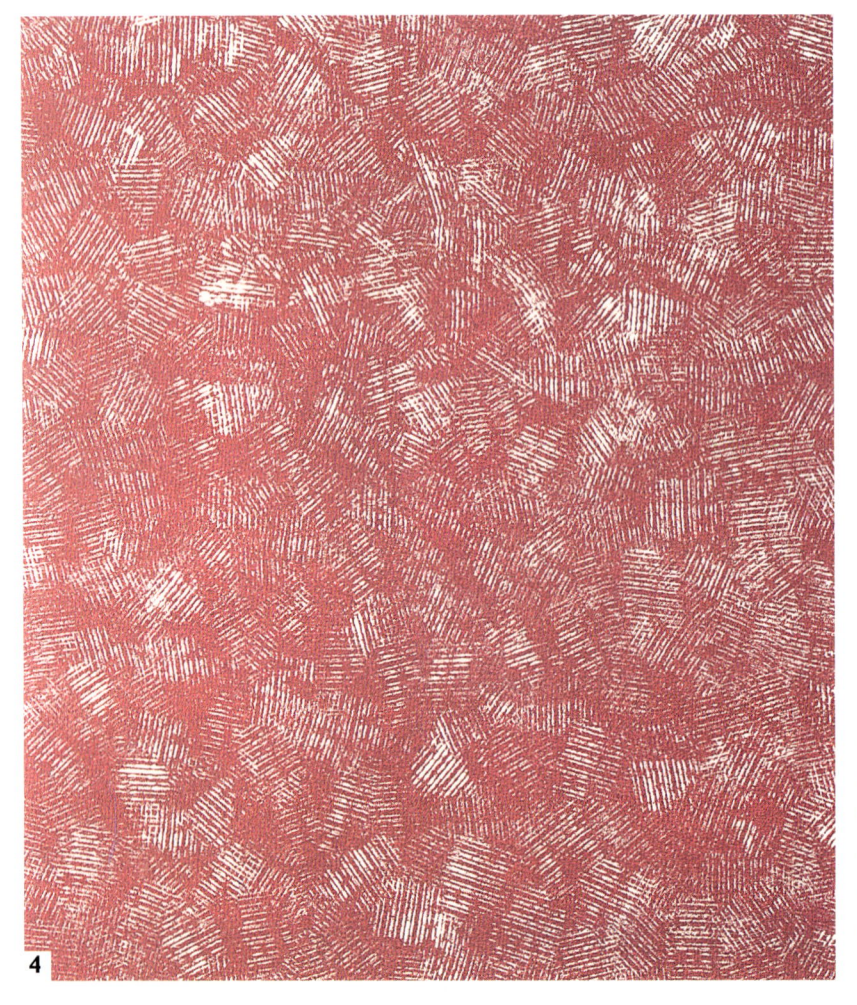

**4.** You can vary this finish by applying a dark colour over a light base or by using a different kind of corduroy. (Note, however, that needlecord is not recommended; it is probably too thin to supply enough pattern.)

"TEXTURED" WALL FINISHES

## CORDUROY RAGGING OFF

### RECIPE
**CORDUROY RAGGING OFF**

**LEVEL OF EXPERTISE:**

**RECOMMENDED ON:** Walls, panelling, cabinetry, furniture, accessories

**NOT RECOMMENDED ON:** Highly carved surfaces

**NUMBER OF PEOPLE:** 1 or 2, depending on project size

**TOOLS:** Newspapers or dust sheets; paint tray; paint stirrers; roller to apply base coat and glaze; white spirit; face mask; rubber gloves; rags for touch up and clean up; corduroy, cut into 30cm squares; pinking shears and lint roller to prepare corduroy

◆ **BASE COAT:** Bone silk-finish emulsion paint

◆ **GLAZE:** Putty transparent oil glaze and artists' oil paint

**VARNISH:** Optional

---

Before you read any further, look back at the final shot of the recipe on the previous page, "Corduroy Ragging On". Now look at the finished effect for this recipe. You can't get a much clearer example of what a change in colour and a switch from the "additive" to the "subtractive" method of applying glaze will do to a painted finish.

The tool for both finishes is the same: corduroy. But this finish is much more subtle for two reasons: the closer colour relationship between the more neutral bone base coat and putty glaze, and the way the glaze is applied. Instead of printing it directly onto the surface with the corduroy, as in the previous recipe, you apply the glaze subtractive style. First, apply it over the base coat with a roller, then use your tool (the corduroy) to lift some of it off.

Note that you can get different effects by using other kinds of corduroy: narrow rib, wide rib, etc. (Needlecord is probably too thin to provide enough pattern.)

When working with cloth, be extra careful. It can fray and cause bits of fuzz to get into your finish. See the "Corduroy Ragging On" recipe for the best way to make corduroy into a good painting tool.

Watch how you hold the corduroy. To get clear imprints, create a flat surface to remove glaze with; bunch the rest of the cloth in your hand, gathering the ends into your palm.

Ragging off will give you a smoother, more sophisticated look. But keep in mind that, especially on a large surface, it is easiest to do with two people—one to roll on the glaze and the other to remove the glaze before it dries. If you're tackling a project alone, you definitely want to work with oil-based glazes because they take longer to dry and thus give you more time for the glaze removal process.

1. Remove fluff from corduroy with masking tape or lint roller.

**THE RECIPES** 141

# CORDUROY RAGGING OFF

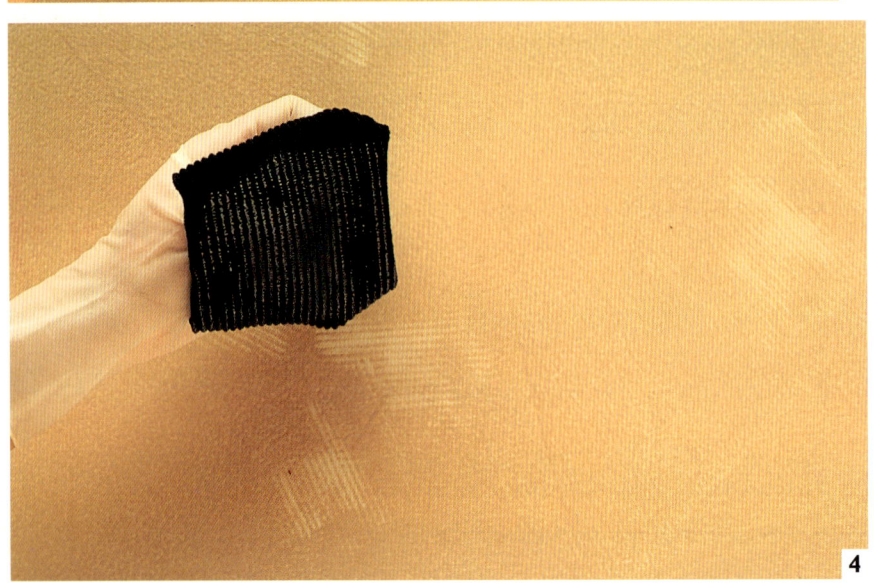

2. Pour glaze into paint tray. Apply glaze over base coat with roller, criss-crossing strokes to get an even finish.

3. Arrange corduroy in hand to form flat surface. Touch lightly to surface to remove glaze. When cloth is in air, shift hand to get a variety of imprints. Work with same rag until saturated (i. e., when it begins putting glaze back on wall instead of removing it). Then change to new rag, and repeat steps 2 and 3.

4. Work in floor-to-ceiling strips of 60 to 90cm. (If you find glaze drying too fast to rag, do smaller sections.) Touch cloth to wall randomly throughout section so that you remove some glaze from all areas when cloth is cleanest. This will keep you from getting a distracting "light spot" in just one area. Stand back regularly to see that smooth overall pattern is developing. But, accept imperfections: reworking them will remove too much glaze. One rag should last for medium-size wall, but have extras on hand so that you don't run the risk of running out.

5. The finished effect, especially in a room filled with window treatments, furnishings, and accessories, will mask surface imperfections.

CORDUROY RAGGING OFF

## PLASTIC-WRAP RAGGING OFF

### RECIPE

**PLASTIC-WRAP RAGGING OFF**

**LEVEL OF EXPERTISE:**

**RECOMMENDED ON:** Walls

**NOT RECOMMENDED ON:** Small surfaces

**NUMBER OF PEOPLE:** 1 or 2, depending on project size

**TOOLS:** Newspapers or dust sheets; paint tray; paint stirrers; roller to apply base coat; brush to apply glaze; white spirit; face mask; rubber gloves; rags for touch up and clean up; rolls of plastic wrap (industrial size for large projects)

◆ **BASE COAT:** Dove white silk-finish emulsion paint

◆ **GLAZE:** Transparent oil glaze and rose artists' oil paint

**VARNISH:** Optional

Through a combination of brush strokes and impressions left by strips of plastic wrap, this finish can give you a pleasing interplay of lights and darks that conveys three-dimensionality.

This finish is a cousin of the leather look you saw in Chapter Nine. However, it has a much stronger "sense of direction", or flow, thanks in part to the way you apply the glaze here—with a brush, all in one direction, instead of with a roller, in several directions.

If you're doing a whole room, you might want to get industrial size rolls of plastic wrap, available at restaurant supply stores. They make it easier for you to roll out the long strips you'll want for this technique.

You can reuse the same strip of plastic wrap a few times—but not too many because it quickly becomes saturated and stops removing paint.

One important point: if you remove the plastic, and there just isn't enough pattern, you can go back over it with a rag or small piece of plastic wrap while the glaze is still wet. Hold the plastic or rag in the same direction as your finish, and remove more glaze. Work slowly and step back from your surface often so that you can see that you're creating a strong pattern of lights and darks.

1. **Over dry base coat, apply glaze with brush. You can apply glaze vertically or horizontally, depending on how you want the "stripes" in the finish to go. Vary pressure as you paint on glaze to create lighter and darker areas that will add depth to your final finish.**

2. **Cut off a long strip of plastic wrap and, starting at bottom of wall, stick plastic to glaze. Work your way up wall, smoothing plastic on, but leaving enough "play" in plastic to create crinkles. If you're working by yourself, you'll need to climb up a ladder, keeping hold of plastic, until you reach the ceiling, and then press plastic firmly in place. If you're working in a pair, station one person on ladder and pass plastic strip up.**

3. **Peel off plastic strip, and stand back to see effect. Adjust your technique on next strip, if needed—i.e., create more crinkles in plastic, press plastic more firmly, etc.**

4. **Starting from edge of first strip, apply either the plastic strip you just removed or use a new strip next to the first, depending on how paint-saturated the plastic is. Repeat process over entire surface.**

PLASTIC-WRAP RAGGING OFF

1

2

3

4

THE RECIPES 145

# PLASTIC BAG RAGGING OFF

## RECIPE

### PLASTIC BAG RAGGING OFF

**LEVEL OF EXPERTISE:**

**RECOMMENDED ON:** Walls, panelling, ceilings, cabinetry, furniture, accessories

**NOT RECOMMENDED ON:** Highly carved surfaces

**NUMBER OF PEOPLE:** 1

**TOOLS:** Newspapers or dust sheets; paint tray; paint stirrers; roller to apply base coat; brush to apply glaze; white spirit; face mask; rubber gloves; rags for touch up and clean up; plastic bags

**BASE COAT:** Robin's egg blue silk-finish emulsion paint

**GLAZE:** Transparent oil glaze and Oxide of Chromium artists' oil paint

**VARNISH:** Optional

---

Here's the traditional "subtractive" technique of ragging off executed with an nontraditional material—plastic sandwich bags. The bags give you a finish with extra depth and a more pronounced texture than you would get if you used the soft cotton rags usually associated with this technique.

Working with plastic has its advantages. For one, the bags are easier to crumple up in your hand than cloth. And you don't have to prepare them like you do cloth—they come out of the box fluff-free and cut to size. Because plastic doesn't absorb glaze like cloth does, however, you'll need more of them than you would cloth. And keep in mind the effect changing bags will have on your finish: a fresh bag will lift off more glaze, so don't make all of your marks with a new bag in one spot.

Remember that because this is a subtractive technique—glaze is applied over the base coat with a paint roller, then removed with the plastic bags—it is best executed by two. However, for a small project, you can go it alone.

A major contributor to the depth and richness of the finish pictured here is the colour. The warm green glaze, with a hint of the blue base coat peeking through, is a great example of what decorative painting has to offer over flat-painted surfaces.

The glowing colour that results when the eye combines the transparent layers of this finish would be a wonderful complement to the deep red, blue, and green hues of a "jewel tone" colour scheme or a gentlemen's club interior, either for the main elements like the walls or on eye-catching accents.

1. Pour glaze into paint tray. Apply over base coat with roller, criss-crossing your strokes to get an even finish.

## PLASTIC BAG RAGGING OFF

**2.** Crumple plastic bag in your hand so that you have a lot of wrinkles in part of bag that will touch surface. Press bag lightly to surface to remove glaze. When bag is off surface, turn your wrist, and sometimes your arm, to vary impressions made in glaze.

**3.** Work in floor-to-ceiling strips about 60 to 90cm wide. (If glaze dries too fast, do smaller sections.) Use same bag until saturated; when it stops removing glaze from surface, use another bag. Touch bag to wall randomly throughout section so that you remove some glaze from all areas when bag is cleanest and thus removes most.

**4.** Stand back to check if pattern is developing evenly. Don't rework sections; you will remove too much glaze. In the finished effect, small imperfections blend in.

**THE RECIPES** 147

## SPATTERING IN FOUR COLOURS

### RECIPE
#### SPATTERING IN FOUR COLOURS

**LEVEL OF EXPERTISE:**

**RECOMMENDED ON:** Walls

**NUMBER OF PEOPLE:** 1

**TOOLS:** Newspapers or dust sheets; paint tray; paint stirrers; roller to apply base coat; face mask; rubber gloves; rags for touch up and clean up; heavy-duty stripping tool and pads

**BASE COAT:** Butter silk-finish emulsion paint

**APPLIED FINISH:** Silk-finish emulsion in 4 colours

- Sunflower
- Dusty rose
- Robin's egg blue
- Teal

**VARNISH:** Optional

---

Need a quick-and-clever way to liven up a child's room? Try this recipe for spattering in a bunch of bright hues. Set against a lively yellow ground, the four colours used here—sunflower, dusty rose, robin's egg blue, and teal—convey youthful exuberance without screaming "children's room". The finish can be a more sophisticated alternative to juvenile wallcovering in a room filled with furnishings in primary colours—one that a child won't outgrow as fast and that can more easily accommodate changes in decor.

This recipe also offers another example of how something you might have around the house can help give you an original finish with ease. Nancy isn't quite certain what made her decide to experiment with a heavy-duty paint-stripping pad, but we're glad she did. Her unusual choice of a painting tool, readily available in paint, hardware, and DIY stores, let her create the appealing finish you see here.

Her technique is actually a cross between two classic decorative-painting techniques—spattering and stippling—but much faster and easier than either of them, especially on large surfaces. And compared to traditional methods of spattering, this one is neater—glaze doesn't fly all over when you dab it on like this, compared to when you bang or flick it off the bristles of a brush.

Note that you can get a similar effect from the kind of brush you use to clean an outdoor grill. But before you go and buy one, maybe you should check what else you have around the house. you never know what kind of finish you might come up with!

Bright hues aren't the only colours this finish looks great in. Take a look at our second "serving suggestion", "Blue Spatter Finish" as shown in a range of blues on page 150. It's a perfect foil to the perennially popular blue-and-white decorating scheme. But don't stop there. This simple-to-achieve effect offers myriad possibilities.

One last tip: when executing this finish, have patience. It does not acquire all its "oomph" until the end. It builds up gradually, layer upon layer, and the final result is enhanced by the way your eye visually "mixes" all those dots of colour.

## SPATTERING IN FOUR COLOURS

1. Pour first emulsion colour into paint tray. Dip stripping tool straight down into glaze. Dab off excess glaze on top of paint tray and on paper until imprints have "spattered" look.

2. Touch tool to wall, straight on, repeatedly. Working in 90cm sections, make imprints over section randomly so that imprints made when tool has most paint on it are spread throughout.

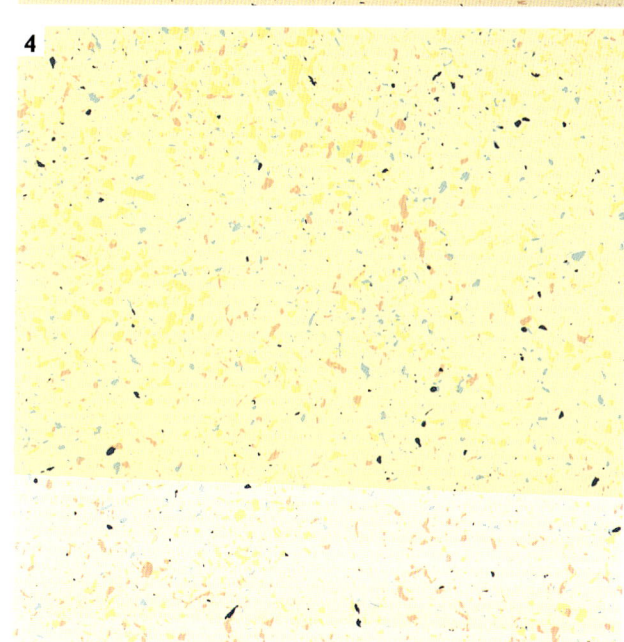

3. Repeat process with second, third, and fourth emulsion glaze colours, cleaning or changing pad on stripping tool between each one. Because the amount you're applying is minute, glazes dry quickly, so you don't have to wait before beginning the next spattering layer.

4. Step back as you work to ensure you are creating an even pattern over your surface.

**THE RECIPES**  149

## SPATTERING

### SERVING SUGGESTION
#### BLUE SPATTER FINISH

If collecting blue-and-white china is your passion, or if you like that "summer house" feeling all year round, you'll love this soft and subtle version of the spattered finish. Done in four shades of blue, from dark to light, it can be the perfect foil for furnishings, window treatments, and accessories with a blue-and-white theme. For tools, step-by-step instructions, etc., see "Spattering In Four Colours", page 148.

**BASE COAT:** White linen silk-finish emulsion paint

**APPLIED FINISH:** 4 matt emulsion paint colours

◆ Sail blue

◆ Cornflower

◆ Navy

◆ Delft blue

150 "TEXTURED" WALL FINISHES

# FLOGGING

## RECIPE

### FLOGGING

**LEVEL OF EXPERTISE:**

**RECOMMENDED ON:** Walls

**NUMBER OF PEOPLE:** 2 recommended, but can be done with 1

**TOOLS:** Newspapers or dust sheets; rags; rollers to apply base coat and glaze; paint trays; paint stirrers; white spirit; face mask; rubber gloves; containers for mixing glazes in; flogging brush or 5cm house-painting brush with extra-long bristles; 2.5cm foam brush

◆ **BASE COAT:** White linen silk-finish emulsion paint

**GLAZES:** Transparent oil glaze and 2 oil-based eggshell paints

◆ Mustard

◆ Brown

**VARNISH:** Optional

---

This technique is a good example of how one decorative finish can lead to another. "Flogging" is an intriguing effect in its own right; but it is also the background for "Leopard Skin", which you'll find in the *Stencilling* chapter. "Flogging" creates a "furry" background over which to apply the leopard's stencilled spots.

Having the right tool for the job is often the key to success. But here, the right tool could easily break the budget. It is called a "flogging" brush, and what makes it special are its 12cm bristles. In this technique, you manipulate the glaze by striking the surface with your brush; the bristles on a flogging brush are long enough so that you don't get the mark of the metal band that holds the bristles in place. As a substitute, choose a much-less-expensive 5cm house-painting brush with the longest bristles you can find.

This recipe would be much more difficult to execute with water-based glazes. Oil-based glazes stay wet much longer and give you enough time to manipulate them.

The depth of this finish comes from the range in opacity of your glazes. You'll use several, from brown glaze comprising mostly glazing liquid to brown paint right from the can. In all cases, apply only a little glaze at a time.

If you are creating this finish to "stand alone", you, of course, have total freedom in its look. But if it will be the background for "Leopard Skin", study the photo of "Leopard Skin" shown on page 172 first. You want to capture the "furry" feeling.

The surface needs to be spotty, but there doesn't need to be any pattern to it. Patches should vary in size. Stand back to check if your light and dark areas fall in pleasing ways. There are actually two distinct flogging stages to this recipe. If you aren't using this as a background for leopard skin, you may prefer to stop after step 3. This gives you a more pronounced "random-brushed" effect with stronger contrasts among glaze colours. Following the rest of the steps on these pages will give a smoother, softer, more fully blended finish.

**THE RECIPES**

## FLOGGING

1. With a roller, apply mustard glaze to surface. Then, while glaze is still wet, start at top of surface and "drag" a 5cm house-painting brush down over glaze. Then, "flog" glaze in rows, starting at the botom of the surface and working upwards. ("Flog" means to hit or beat the surface quickly with the side of the bristle of the brush.) Let dry thoroughly.

2. Mix about four brown glazes, using the same colour paint but varying the amount of glazing liquid from mostly glazing liquid to brown paint straight from can. Using just a little glaze at a time, apply paint in patches by dabbing tip and sides of 2.5cm foam brush on surface.

152  "TEXTURED" WALL FINISHES

FLOGGING

3. Immediately "flog" paint patches with 5cm house-painting brush. Vary size of patches. Be sure to leave some mustard glaze visible.

4. Working with foam brush in one hand and house-painting brush in other hand, apply more of each brown glaze in same manner, but taking off less paint. Instead of patting the surface, just brush it lightly. Let dry thoroughly. To continue with "Leopard Skin" recipe, turn to page 173.

THE RECIPES   153

# CHAPTER ELEVEN

# SMALL-SURFACE SPECIALTIES & STENCILLING

What do you do if you love antique furniture, but can't afford to buy period pieces? What do you do if you've always wanted fine mouldings or charming handpainted designs gracing your home? You don't have to be an artist to achieve the beautiful results found on the following pages.

Three traditional techniques can add classic looks and fine details to worn or dated surroundings. Two are small-surface specialties—découpage and crackle glazing—that can transform ordinary objects into new family heirlooms. The third, stencilling, offers an easy and affordable substitute for wall-paper or fine mouldings, and can give plain furniture an appealing folk-art look.

But these recipes can do more than antique: They can also be used to create the most modern styles, just by using updated patterns and colours.

While working with these techniques is easy, painting the overall paint coats on some objects and furniture may prove challenging for the novice decorative painter. Take preparation work seriously—in decorative painting, it's a major part of your end result. Although the crackle glaze can hide, and in some cases even be enhanced by, surface imperfections, too many might cause the finish to peel. And with découpage, your pasted-on designs might not adhere properly. See Chapter Three, *Preparing To Paint*, for additional help in this area. Also make sure you have paint that is compatible with your piece.

Oil-based paint is considered more durable and, therefore, recommended for pieces such as chairs, that will be often used. Varnish also serves as a finish protector on pieces you'll handle daily. See *Mixing Paints* for further guidance.

**Through decorative painting, a simple shape like this pedestal can be transformed into something just as special as the object that it displays.**

SMALL-SURFACE SPECIALTIES & STENCILLING

# CRACKLE GLAZE

## RECIPE

### CRACKLE GLAZE

**LEVEL OF EXPERTISE:**

**RECOMMENDED ON:** Furniture, accessories, moulding, cabinetry

**NOT RECOMMENDED ON:** Floors

**NUMBER OF PEOPLE:** 1

**TOOLS:** Newspaper or dust sheets; power sander; abrasive paper; tacky rag; paint tray; paint stirrers; white spirit to clean up oil-based coat; water to clean up emulsion paint and crackle glaze; face mask; rubber gloves; 3cm nylon sash brush for glazing; 3cm Chinese bristle brush for base coat

◆ **BASE COAT:** Palamino brown oil-based eggshell paint

◆ **APPLIED FINISH:** Layer of water-based crackle glaze (see *Sources*, page 185), then layer of hazelnut emulsion paint

**VARNISH:** Use oil-based varnish

---

That much-sought-after "patina of age" made easy—that's what this finish is all about. Here, a junk shop find takes on the persona of a prized antique with an off-the-shelf glazing product and a few simple steps.

Remember, however, that the piece you choose to work on must be in good condition to merit such a transformation, because although the process is not difficult, it is time consuming—especially all the sanding it sometimes takes to get a piece ready. Before you transform anything, be sure it is structurally sound.

Also consider that if this is your first attempt at painting furniture, you may want to do a practice run on something smaller. Consider buying a small unpainted wooden box, like those you can buy at craft shops, to test your skills on first.

There are recipes for making your own crackle glaze but, as this project shows, off-the-shelf products work perfectly well. If, however, you can't find ready-made crackle glaze in paint or hobby shops in your area, you may be able to get one through mail order (see *Sources*).

To get results like you see here, you can just use the glaze straight from the tin. For finer cracks, you can thin the molasses-like glaze from its gummy state to the consistency of syrup (but no thinner) with water. Thinning the glaze will cause it to drip even more than it's already inclined to do; but don't worry—the drips won't show much because of the crackled surface.

What causes the cracks is no deep, dark secret, but rather a common effect one usually tries to avoid. You can get a similarly cracked surface—although not as consistently—just by applying a water-based paint over an oil-based paint.

Colourwise, you'll probably get the best success by using a lighter and darker shade of the same colour. Either the lighter or darker shade can be the base coat; experiment to see which you prefer.

One last tip—if you do use two colours close in tone, and you want to give your work a true "antiqued" look, go with optional step 3: before you varnish, use a cotton rag to rub on a thin layer of your base coat in places to create a distressed look.

To begin, paint your base coat. (Remember to paint underside of the chair.) Let dry completely; overnight, if possible. Then sand piece (with power sander or by hand, depending on size of piece), and wipe with a tacky rag to ensure next coat will adhere.

**THE RECIPES** 157

# CRACKLE GLAZE

158 SMALL-SURFACE SPECIALTIES & STENCILLING

CRACKLE GLAZE

1. Paint on crackle glaze in smooth layer. Let dry thoroughly (overnight).

2. Apply coat of emulsion paint. Crackling will begin almost immediately. Smooth paint on with easy, sweeping strokes, painting in direction of wood grain as much as possible. Avoid going back over your work. Let dry thoroughly (overnight is recommended).

3. If you wish, use a cotton rag to rub on random patches of your base coat colour for a more "aged" look.

4. With paint pad, apply coat of water-based varnish to ensure durable finish. Finished effect gives an antiqued feel.

THE RECIPES

## DÉCOUPAGE

### RECIPE

**DÉCOUPAGE**

**LEVEL OF EXPERTISE:**

**RECOMMENDED ON:** Furniture, cabinetry, accessories including trays, boxes, screens, lamps

**NOT RECOMMENDED ON:** Floors, highly carved surfaces

**NUMBER OF PEOPLE:** 1

**TOOLS:** Newspaper or dust sheets; small power sander; abrasive paper; tacky rag; paint tray; paint stirrers; white spirit; face mask; rubber gloves; 30cm square cotton rags; low-tack masking tape; small artist's bristle brush for putting in lines; pictures to paste down; scissors or craft knife to cut out pictures; pencil or chalk marker; white glue; toothpicks and/or fine paint brush to apply glue to back of pictures

**BASE COAT:** Almond spray paint

**GLAZE:** Transparent oil glaze and white artists' oil paint

**LINING:** Dark green oil-based paint

**VARNISH:** Use oil-based varnish

Handpainted furniture is so popular today, but what if you can't paint? In this recipe, you'll learn one way to get the look.

This recipe borrows a technique from history: découpage. In 18th-century Europe, découpage regularly stood in for hand-painting on fashionable lacquered furniture, and it became a favourite pastime among craft-loving Victorian women.

Although easier by far than painting on decoration, découpage isn't just fun and games. With this technique, neatness counts. How carefully you cut out your shapes, how meticulously you prepare your surface, and how well you apply the several coats of varnish required will determine your end result.

These wood nesting tables, a junk shop find, required good surface preparation. The tables were sanded, first with a small power sander and then by hand, and wiped with a tacky rag to remove particles, the scourge of decorative painting. The investment of time and energy was well worth it because the smoother your surface, the better the finish looks and the more durable the finish is because subsequent paint layers find it easier to adhere. (For a more detailed guide to surface preparation, see Chapter Three.)

The almond-coloured base coat demonstrates another way to apply paint: it was sprayed on. Over that is a decorative finish called "ragging on". One of the simplest techniques, it is the same method used in "Corduroy Ragging On", and plays a role in several other recipes in this book.

A good idea when picking background colours for your découpage project is to take a cue from the background colour of the motifs you cut out and do a mottled-colour (i.e., ragged, sponged, marbled, etc.) version of that. Note, however, that traditionally découpage was done on a plain painted background, and you can easily do the same.

For this particular découpage project, the arrangement of the flower shapes plays a big role in its appeal. But, if you're concerned your "artistic eye" isn't yet up to it, you might prefer to use simpler shapes and place them randomly.

In your search for just the right motifs, check out old books, gift wrap, greeting cards, old-fashioned valentines, playing cards, cotton fabrics, and black-and-white or colour photographs. Using matchbook covers, postcards, or even business cards could turn a table into a memory keeper. If you want to use pictures from magazines or newspapers, however, be sure to test first; applying glue and varnish to the thin paper may make the image on the back of the picture show through.

Varnishing is at the heart of this technique. You'll apply numerous coats to protect your handiwork. There are a number of varnishes you can use, but water-based has its advantages. For one thing, it's easy to clean up. And it's semi-matt; many oil-based varnishes give surfaces a high shine that you may not want for your project.

## DÉCOUPAGE

**1.** Prepare surface by sanding and then remove particles with tack cloth. Spray paint almond base coat and let dry. In paint tray, mix 20 per cent white oil-based eggshell paint and 80 per cent glazing liquid; thin to consistency of milk. Crumple 30cm square cotton rag loosely in your hand. Dip rag in glaze, and dab off on paper, testing impression. Touch rag lightly to table or object, "ragging on" over entire surface. Let dry overnight.

**2.** With low-tack masking tape, cover areas you don't want to get paint on, then paint in lines with dark green oil-based paint and small flat bristle brush, using small, short strokes. Paint over edge of tape to be sure you don't miss any spots. Press tape into place firmly to prevent seepage. But be prepared for seepage by having your base colour on hand for touch ups. (Note: on this piece, lines are recessed and thus easier to paint; so extensive masking wasn't required.) Let dry thoroughly.

**THE RECIPES** 161

DÉCOUPAGE

**3**

**4**

**5**

SMALL-SURFACE SPECIALTIES & STENCILLING

6

3. With craft knife or scissors, cut out pictures you will use for découpage. Before applying glue, lay out pieces to see where you want them to go and mark their positions very lightly on your surface.

4. Mix a little water into glue so that it spreads more easily. Apply glue to back of pictures with paint brush or toothpick, depending on size of piece. Press pictures in place. Let dry. Make sure they are perfectly flat.

5. Apply three to ten coats of varnish to pieces, sanding lightly and wiping with tacky rag between coats for better adherence. Let dry thoroughly between coats.

6. The découpage technique lets you get a hand-painted look even if you're not an artist.

# A Guide to Stencilling

## WHICH STENCILLING PROJECT TO DO

Stencilling is easy, but it can also be time consuming. What takes the most time are multi-colour stencils—such as the architectural moulding—because for each colour you must cut and work with an additional stencil. Before you start, decide how much time you can invest, keeping in mind that you can get great results in good time with a single-colour motif—like the tile design included here.

With multi-colour stencils, you must also pay strict attention to registration—the way each stencil aligns on top of the previous one. This is crucial to a professional look. To make this happen, in each stencil, you will cut out registration marks that help keep the alignment precise. Be sure to paint in those marks before starting on the rest of the stencil.

## USING THE STENCILS IN THIS BOOK

You'll find patterns for each of the stencils starting on page 178. Just enlarge or reduce them to the size you need for your project on a photocopy machine.

Next, transfer the patterns to either acetate or stencilling cardboard, both available at craft shops and some art stores. Which material to use depends on the project you select. In each recipe, a material is specified. Substitutions are perfectly permissible—although with multi-colour stencils, see-through acetate makes alignment easier. See the next page for step-by-step instructions on transferring and cutting out stencils on both acetate and cardboard.

Cutting stencils can be tricky, especially if there are lots of curved lines and little "bridges", those small areas that hold the elements of your pattern together.

Practise first. Nancy found that a new electric stencil-cutting tool, called a heat pen (see stockists page), made the job much easier; she demonstrates it on the next page. (See *Sources*, page 185, for stockist.)

Two tips: use masking tape to mend your stencil if you make a mistake. And for rounded edges, you might find it a bit easier to turn the stencil instead of moving your knife.

Especially for multi-colour stencil projects, after cutting out the stencils, you should always number them and mark them with the words "front", "top", and "right". This aids in aligning them properly. (Especially in the heat of the project, mix-ups have been known to occur.)

## CHOOSING PAINTS AND TOOLS

Although you can stencil with other tools—paint brushes, sponges, and spray paint—stencilling brushes are good investments. The popularity of stencilling has made these round brushes with flat bristles much more readily available; check craft and art supply shops, as well as mail-order catalogues (see *Sources*, page 185).

As with regular brushes, stencilling brushes come in a wide range of sizes. The size to choose depends on the size of your project; a larger brush can make a project go faster.

You can buy special stencilling paints, but you can also get good results with emulsion paint or water-based artist's acrylics.

A cardinal rule with stencilling: use only a little paint at a time so that it doesn't seep under the stencil and ruin your design. And note that you can vary the pressure with which you apply the paint to change the look: for instance, you can create a "fade-away" effect by dabbing your brush more firmly at the centre of your design and lightening your touch as you move toward the edges. Experimenting with different brushes and paints will make your stencil look unique.

**KEEPING STENCILS IN PLACE**
A quick tip to make stencilling easier: use low-tack stencilling adhesive spray to keep your stencil in place. If you have a large stencil and find it pulling away from your surface, back up the adhesive with masking tape. Note that when spraying adhesive, you should always wear a protective face mask.

## RECIPE
### TRANSFERRING AND CUTTING A STENCIL FROM CARDBOARD

Using a photocopy machine, make several copies of the pattern you would like to use. You'll only need one copy of each part of the pattern, but it's a good idea to have extra copies on hand in case you make a tough-to-repair mistake in cutting. You can either keep the stencil pattern the same size, reduce it, or enlarge it, depending on the scale of your project.

**TOOLS:** Several photocopies of stencil pattern; cardboard; scissors; low-tack stencilling adhesive spray; craft knife

**Spray adhesive on the back of a photocopy. Press the copy down onto cardboard cut to the width of your stencil. It's easier to leave the cardboard extra long until you've cut out your stencil so that you have something to hold on to. Cut out white areas of the stencil using a craft knife. Be sure to cut out registration marks, if indicated.**

## RECIPE
### TRANSFERRING AND CUTTING A STENCIL FROM ACETATE

**TOOLS:** Photocopies of stencil pattern; acetate, available in rolls or sheets; cardboard, about size of stencil pattern; scissors; low-tack stencilling adhesive spray; piece of window glass; masking tape; electric stencil-cutting tool or craft knife

**Spray adhesive on back of a photocopy trimmed roughly to size of stencil pattern. Place copy on top of cardboard, pressing it into place. Place photocopy under piece of glass. With scissors, cut acetate a little larger than size of stencil. With masking tape, tape acetate down on top of glass, centered over photocopy. Plug in cutting tool. When hot, use it to cut out stencil pattern, moving slowly along outside edge of white elements of design. (See page 175 for tips on cutting along curves.)**

**THE RECIPES** 165

# TILE

## RECIPE
### TILE

**LEVEL OF EXPERTISE:**

**RECOMMENDED ON:** Walls, panelling, floors, borders, fireplace surrounds, countertops, tabletops, furnishings

**NOT RECOMMENDED ON:** Highly carved surfaces

**NUMBER OF PEOPLE:** 1

**TOOLS:** Newspapers or dust sheets; rags; roller for applying base coat; paint tray; paint stirrers; rubber gloves; stencil board; craft knife; cutting board; low-tack stencilling adhesive spray; masking tape; 2.5cm nylon stencilling brush; palette; paper for testing brushes on; spirit level; large foam brush for varnishing

**BASE COAT:** Celery silk-finish emulsion paint

**APPLIED FINISH:** Tan silk-finish emulsion paint

**VARNISH:** Use oil-based varnish

---

Always wanted a tile splashback behind your stove? Why not stencil one in? This original stencilled design easily captures the look and feel of tile. You can use it to cover a wall, border a room, or arranged in a simple group of four, as pictured here, serve as an elegant inset panel.

You'll find the pattern for this stencil on page 178. Just remove it from the book and enlarge or reduce it on a photocopy machine depending on your needs. Then transfer the pattern onto stencilling cardboard and cut it out, following the instructions on page 165. Mark on stencil the words "front", "top", and "right" so that it can be aligned easily each time. (See page 164 for additional guidelines.)

A big plus with this design: you only use one stencil so you don't have to align another stencil precisely on top of it. And since this interlocking pattern is a simple repeat, you just move the stencil over and put it down the same way each time.

To line up your stencilling for smaller projects, you'll need just a spirit level and masking tape. Apply horizontal and vertical lines of tape to the surface where you want your stencilling to be, then adjust the tape using the level until the lines are straight.

With that method, you avoid marking your surface. For an entire room, however, you'll need to draw in pencil or chalk guidelines. Put them in as lightly as possible (you may need to paint over the pencil after stencilling).

1. Spray adhesive on back of stencil. Put up masking tape guidelines, checking them with spirit level.

2. Flatten stencil carefully against wall, lining it up against bottom edge of tape line you applied to your surface. Put paint on palette. Dab stencilling brush lightly in paint, then dab on paper until brush is almost dry. Dab brush over stencil, covering surface thoroughly. Lift off stencil and, orientated the same way, place down next to first print; repeat process until your surface is completed.

3. Arranged in a simple group of four, the stencil becomes an elegant insert panel.

TILE

THE RECIPES    167

# GRAPE-LEAF MOTIF

## RECIPE

### GRAPE-LEAF MOTIF

**LEVEL OF EXPERTISE:**

**RECOMMENDED ON:** Walls, panelling, floors, ceilings, door and window surrounds, fireplace surrounds, furnishings, accessories

**NOT RECOMMENDED ON:** Highly carved surfaces

**NUMBER OF PEOPLE:** 1

**TOOLS:** Newspapers or dust sheets; rags for touch up; paint stirrers; paint tray; low-tack masking tape to hold stencil in place; rubber gloves; one 30 x 45cm piece of acetate for main stencil, plus 5 smaller pieces for detail stencils; craft knife; cutting board; 2 stencilling brushes, 2.5cm or larger; 2 palettes; paper for testing on

◇ **BASE COAT:** Dove white matt emulsion paper

**GLAZES:** For ragged background—50 per cent emulsion and 50 per cent water—2 colours

◇ Pearl

◇ Sky blue

**\*STENCIL PAINT:** matt emulsion paint (5 "grape" colours)—

◆ Royal violet

◆ Heather

◆ Lavender

◆ Blue ink

◆ Tapestry wine

4 shades of green—

◆ Basil

◆ Indian

◆ Hunter

◆ Thicket

**VARNISH:** Optional

*Paint stores may sell you 250 ml "tester pots" or you can match the colours up to specialist stencil paints.

---

Love the hand-painted look, but don't consider yourself an artist? No problem. Use this stencil as a jumping-off point.

The stencil—consisting of a main pattern and several smaller elements (leaves, grapevine)—gives you the basic forms and helps you keep those forms consistent throughout your project—often a challenge for beginning painters. (For instance, if you're framing a doorway, it can ensure that the first leaves you paint, on one side of the doorway, will look like the last leaves you paint, on the other side.)

Then, by stencilling over the shapes in several colours instead of one, you can easily give your design a sense of depth. There's no reason stencilling has to be "flat"; the building-up adds interest and makes a design unique.

Finally, by painting in simple details, such as wavy lines for veining on leaves, you can capture the hand-done look. To see how far you can go with this, turn to the photo of the designer showhouse room on page 116. Nancy and Jeffrey Brooks, the interior designer of the room, assisted Nick Devlin, the mural painter, by stencilling in individual leaf shapes for the background of the grapevine. Nick went over every leaf, hand-painting in detail on the stencilling and filling in the grapevine structure and background. (For another look at how to hand-paint veining, see the *"Fantasy" Marbling* chapter.)

This stencil is a charmer. It features one of today's most fashionable motifs: fruit designs.

SMALL-SURFACE SPECIALTIES & STENCILLING

## GRAPE-LEAF MOTIF

Another part of the stencil's charm comes from its free-flowing nature. It is especially fun to do because it is much less rigid. You don't need to register it or arrange it in a straight row, and you can put the next motif wherever you want. For instance, you can apply all or parts of the main motif to walls randomly (instead of evenly spaced or in rows) to create your own original wallcovering.

The pattern for this stencil is on page 179. Enlarge or reduce them on a photocopy machine, if needed, to fit your space. Then transfer the patterns to acetate and cut them out.

Because you'll want to flip the stencil over and use it on the other side to get different angles, don't spray the back with stencilling adhesive to hold it in place. Use low-tack masking tape.

The instructions for this recipe include how to paint the "sky" background. You can, of course, put this stencil over any background, whether solid or "broken" colour or plain wood.

To get a cloudy look, make the blue and white paint for the sky very transparent by watering it down to a 50/50 mix with water. And apply paint by dabbing it lightly on your surface with a sea sponge, preferably one with a lot of holes in it.

(Note: this technique is called "sponging on." For more tips on sponging on, see the "Stucco" recipe and the *Fantasy Marbling* chapter. For a detailed review of sponging, see Chapter Five in the first edition of *Recipes for Surfaces*.)

1. In paint tray, mix 50 per cent sky blue emulsion paint and 50 per cent water. Wet sea sponge, and wring out. Dip sponge in paint, then off-load most of paint onto paper. Touch sponge to wall lightly, turning your wrist when sponge is in air to vary impressions. Cover much of pearl base coat with blue. Let paint dry. (This will happen quickly, before you're ready to start your next coat.)

2. In paint tray, mix half pearl emulsion paint and half water. Rinse out sponge, and wring well. Dip in paint, off-load excess on paper. Touch lightly to wall in areas where sky blue is heaviest to bring back some of base-coat colour.

**THE RECIPES**

**3.** With masking tape, position main stencil on wall in your starting position. Prepare palette with four shades of green paint.

**4.** Dab stencil brush into one green colour and blot off excess on paper until brush is almost dry. Dab brush over leaves. Repeat with next three green colours, one on top of the other. (Because you use so little paint, previous colour should be dry by the time you're on to next.)

**5.** Set up palette with five "grape" paint colours. Dab second stencilling brush into one colour, blot off excess on paper, then dab over grapes. Repeat process with other five grape colours. Note: Don't go over every grape in all five colours. Variations enhance the look. Make some more red or purple; even green.

**6.** Remove stencil and move to next spot, taping in place. If you're placing stencil next to first design, you can overlap it slightly; but make sure none of the previous design shows through in the areas you will stencil next. Note: it's not necessary to do all of the next stencil; you may prefer just to do some leaves, or skip one bunch of grapes. Step back and view pattern you're creating.

# GRAPE-LEAF MOTIF

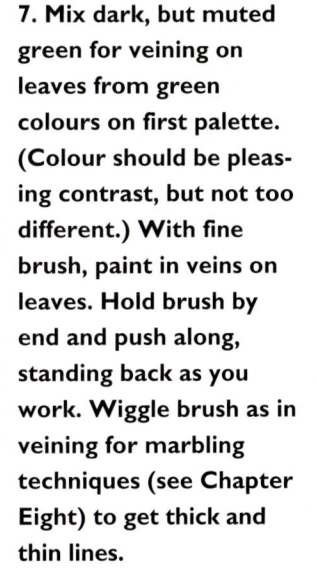

**7.** Mix dark, but muted green for veining on leaves from green colours on first palette. (Colour should be pleasing contrast, but not too different.) With fine brush, paint in veins on leaves. Hold brush by end and push along, standing back as you work. Wiggle brush as in veining for marbling techniques (see Chapter Eight) to get thick and thin lines.

**8.** Using separate detail stencil, put in some grape-vines using medium-green paint.

**9.** Add in separate stencils of leaves where desired—in a corner, for example, where main stencil might not fit. Or, on the floor nearby, as if single leaf had fallen off vine. Then paint in veining.

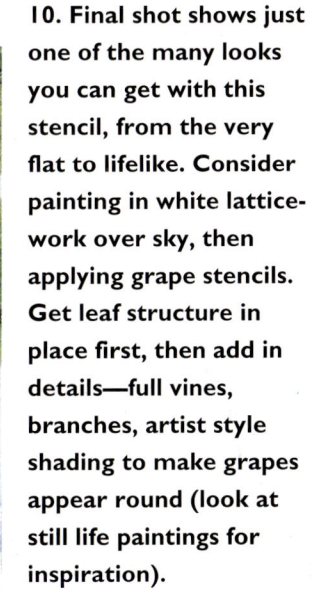

**10.** Final shot shows just one of the many looks you can get with this stencil, from the very flat to lifelike. Consider painting in white lattice-work over sky, then applying grape stencils. Get leaf structure in place first, then add in details—full vines, branches, artist style shading to make grapes appear round (look at still life paintings for inspiration).

THE RECIPES  171

# LEOPARD SKIN

## RECIPE

### LEOPARD SKIN

**LEVEL OF EXPERTISE:**

**RECOMMENDED ON:** Walls, panelling, furnishings, accessories

**NOT RECOMMENDED ON:** Highly carved surfaces

**NUMBER OF PEOPLE:** 1

**TOOLS:** Newspapers or dust sheets; rags for touch up; paint stirrers; white spirit; face mask; rubber gloves; 30 x 45cm sheet of acetate; craft knife; cutting board; removable artist's adhesive spray; masking tape; 2.5cm stencilling brushes; palette; paper for testing brushes on; spirit level

**BASE COAT:** White linen silk-finish emulsion paint and eggshell paint—see "Flogging" recipe, page 151 for colour details.

**STENCILLING:** Chocolate oil-based paint

**GLAZE:** Oil-based glazing liquid and 2 oil based low-lustre paints

◆ Mustard

◆ Brown

**VARNISH:** Optional

---

Exotic animal prints are finding a home in many decorating styles. A wall of stencilled leopard skin might make an ideal backdrop for modern furnishings or the latest revivals. Animal prints are also a natural with "global" settings, those inspired by cultural and ethnic influences from distant corners of the world, as well as "environmental" interiors, which emphasize natural materials and earth tones. And leopard skin accents—from a stencilled tabletop to an old hat-box—sit well with styles as diverse as British Colonial and 1950s.

On page 180, you'll find the pattern for this stencil. Follow the instructions for cutting out a stencil on acetate, a clear material available in sheets or rolls at art or craft stores. (See page 165 for more on cutting out stencils.)

Be sure to cut out the registration marks on the four sides of this stencil; these small notches are vital to lining up your stencil precisely each time. When you move your stencil, don't overlap it.

You can see what a beautiful effect you can get with this stencil from the pictures. But what you can't tell is how easy it is. Usually, to look this good, faux leopard skin needs to have overlapping spots—which would require cutting and using two stencils. Here, you need only one.

The key to this is the background. It's what gives the finish its almost furry look, as well as its range of lights and darks. You'll find the recipe for the background, called "Flogging", in the chapter on *"Textured" Wall Finishes*. That's because the flogged background works so well as a finish in its own right. To get the leopard skin look you see here, start there.

Note that if you can't find acetate, you can cut this stencil out of cardboard. Acetate, however, is easier to work with because you can see through it. Another option is to substitute spray paint for oil-based paint; on a large surface, this would be a time saver.

172 SMALL-SURFACE SPECIALTIES & STENCILLING

# LEOPARD SKIN

1. Wearing face mask and gloves, spray back of stencil with adhesive. Mark guidelines lightly on surface so that the first time you put your stencil down it is straight and level. After that, each time you move stencil, align it with last. (Note: elaborate measuring isn't necessary; pattern hides variations.) Use masking tape, if necessary, to ensure stencil stays in place. Put paint on palette. Dip 2.5cm stencilling brush in paint, then "off-load" extra paint onto test paper or paper plate.

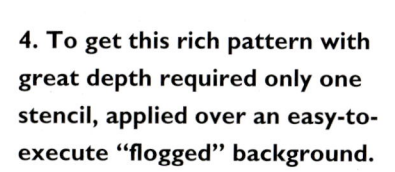

2. Dab brush lightly over surface, filling in stencil pattern. Then move stencil to adjacent spot; put masking tape under registration marks and paint over marks.

3. Repeat stencil process until background is covered. Let dry thoroughly. Paint over registration marks first.

4. To get this rich pattern with great depth required only one stencil, applied over an easy-to-execute "flogged" background.

THE RECIPES   173

# ARCHITECTURAL MOULDING

## RECIPE

### ARCHITECTURAL MOULDING

**LEVEL OF EXPERTISE:**

**RECOMMENDED ON:** Room border at ceiling height

**NOT RECOMMENDED ON:** Floors, small or highly carved surfaces

**NUMBER OF PEOPLE:** 1

**TOOLS:** Newspapers or dust sheets; rags for touch up and clean up; paint tray; paint roller for applying base coat; paint stirrers; rubber gloves; package of cheesecloth, cut into 60cm squares; large sheet of acetate to cut three stencils from; craft knife; cutting board; low-tack stencilling adhesive spray; masking tape; 3 2.5cm nylon stencilling brushes, 1 for each glaze colour; palette; paper for testing

**BASE COAT:** Coffee matt emulsion paint

**APPLIED FINISH:** Matt emulsion paint in 4 colours

- Pearl (for cheeseclothing)
- Latte
- Cappucino
- Espresso

**VARNISH:** Optional

You can find stencils everywhere, but it's not often you see an architectural stencil like this egg-and-dart crown moulding Nancy designed. This stencil can easily stand alone at the ceiling line of a room. Or, if you're lucky enough to have moulding already in place, as shown here, you can use the stencil to add extra character.

Stencilled or otherwise, cornicing can transform a room. It can turn a plain setting into a showcase for classic furnishings. It can make a small, boxy interior seem more spacious by drawing the eye upward.

The colours chosen for this stencil contribute greatly to the finished effect. They help convey a sense of depth by creating highlights and shadows like those you'd find on old moulding carved long ago from stone.

Note that the stencil itself is delicate—i.e., there are lots of curving lines and little "bridges" that connect the parts of the design. Especially for big projects like a large room, have masking tape on hand to repair those bridges along the way.

The background here has been "cheeseclothed", a technique named for the gauzelike material with which glaze is applied. Cheeseclothing is from the "ragging" family of techniques. A range of techniques from that group would work well here, although cheeseclothing is particularly recommended because of the soft, subtle finish it creates. (For a detailed guide to cheeseclothing and related techniques, see the *Cloth Distressing* chapter in the first edition of *Recipes for Surfaces*, page 107.)

You can buy packages of cheesecloth in paint or hardware stores, DIY stores, and sometimes supermarkets (it is used in cooking to strain food). About three packages will be enough for a medium-size wall. Before you begin, wash the cheesecloth on gentle cycle and tumble it dry to give it a softer texture.

The trickiest part of this project is cutting out the three stencils that make up the design. You'll find the patterns on pages 181-182.

# ARCHITECTURAL MOULDING

**1.** Apply masking tape over edge of cornicing to keep any paint from getting on it. Pour paint into paint tray.

**2.** Bunch square of cheesecloth in your hand, tucking in edges to keep threads from getting in paint. Dip in paint, test on paper, then touch cloth to wall repeatedly, turning your wrist and arm so that different parts of the cloth touch the surface and thus create a variety of impressions. When cloth is almost dry, dip in paint again. Repeat process, working in 90cm sections. Stand back from surface often to see overall effect. Apply paint lightly and build up slowly for even finish; avoid creating strong dark or light areas, which will pull the eye away from stencilling.

Follow the directions for transferring and cutting out a stencil on page 165, and see page 164 for additional guidelines. Cutting out these patterns is particularly challenging because of all the curves. Two tips: if you make a mistake, mend it with masking tape. And when cutting a curve, you may find it easier to move your stencil instead of your knife. Be sure to cut out the bow-tie shaped registration marks on the side and bottom of each stencil; lining up the three stencils precisely is key to a professional look, and matching up the marks each time lets you do this.

Once cut, number your stencils and mark on each one (with a spirit marker) the words "front", "up", and "right" so that you can line them up correctly each time. It's easy to get mixed up in the heat of the project.

**THE RECIPES**

ARCHITECTURAL MOULDING

176    SMALL-SURFACE SPECIALTIES & STENCILLING

## ARCHITECTURAL MOULDING

3. Wearing mask and gloves, spray back of first stencil with adhesive. Align first stencil with edge of moulding or ceiling line. Place small pieces of masking tape under each bow-tie shaped registration mark (this prevents paint which is not part of the pattern from getting on surface). Put some of first paint colour on palette. Dip in 2.5cm stencilling brush and dab off excess paint on paper (brush should be almost dry). Dab brush over registration marks first. Then fill in rest of pattern by patting brush firmly over stencil. Remove stencil carefully so that it doesn't rip. (Don't wipe stencils after use; they might rip. Just store flat.) Paint dries quickly; so you don't have to wait before going to next step.

4. Put second paint colour on palette. Spray back of second stencil with adhesive. Using registration marks, align second stencil exactly over first. Dip second brush in paint, test on paper, then pat firmly—first over registration marks, then rest of stencil. Remove stencil carefully.

5. Repeat process, using third paint colour, stencilling brush, and stencil, to complete one design.

6. Put first stencil up next to design you just completed, overlapping it slightly. (Re-spray stencil with adhesive, if needed.) Repeat steps 4 through 7 as many times as necessary to complete your project.

7. The subtle colours of the finished effect help convey a sense of depth.

THE RECIPES

# Tile

# Grape-Leaf Motif

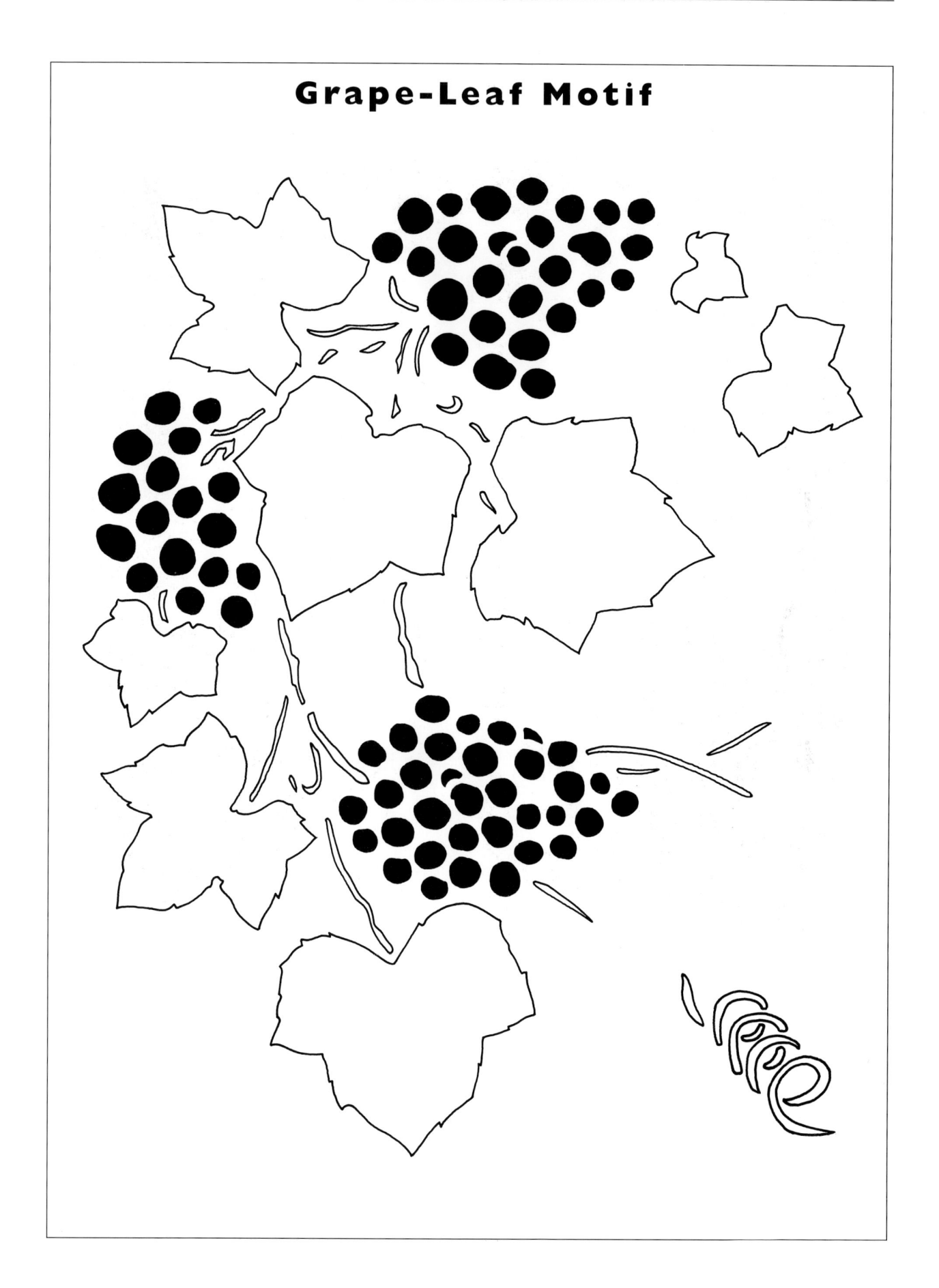

STENCILS

# Leopard skin

# Architectural Moulding

A

B

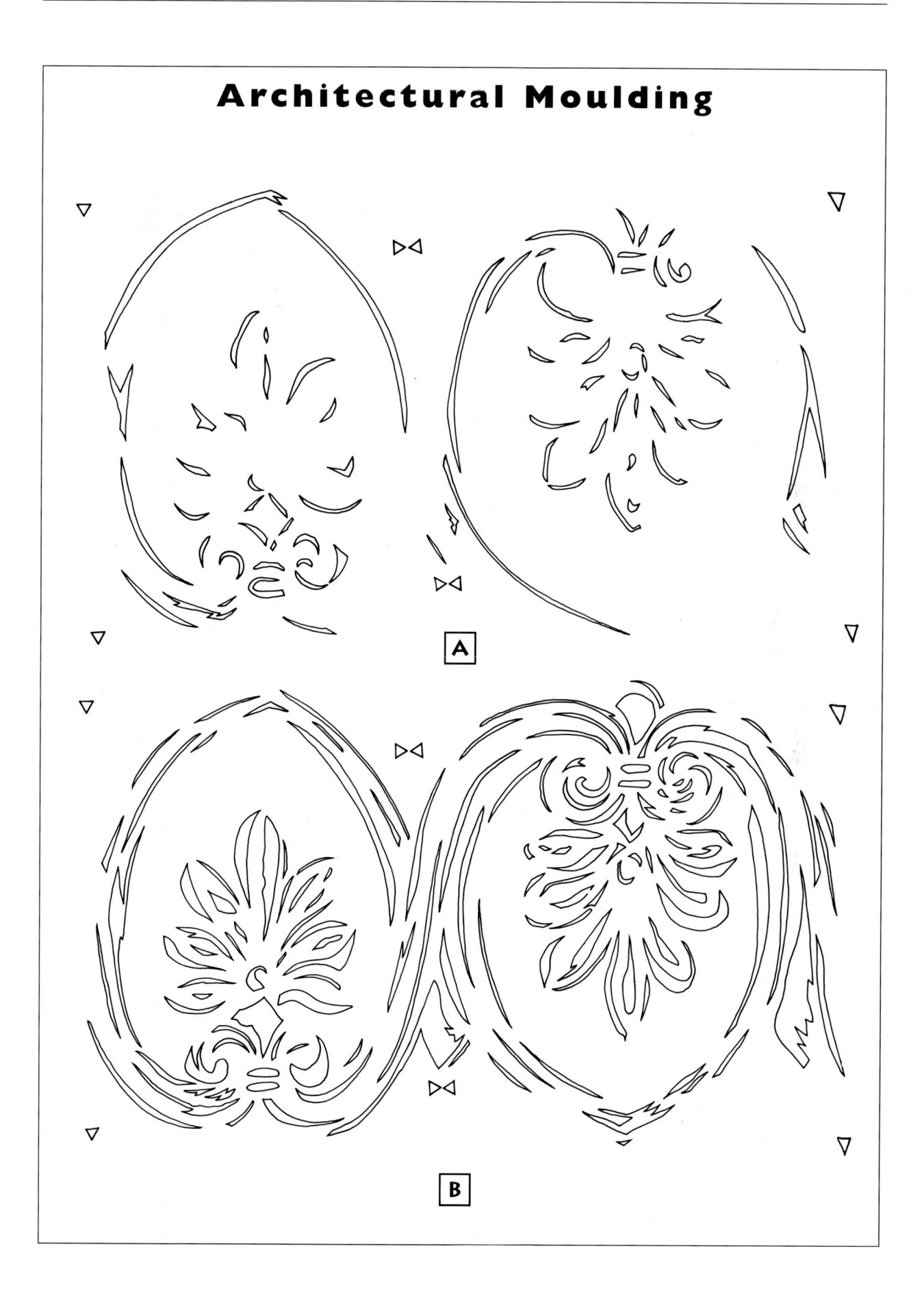

STENCILS 181

# Architectural Moulding

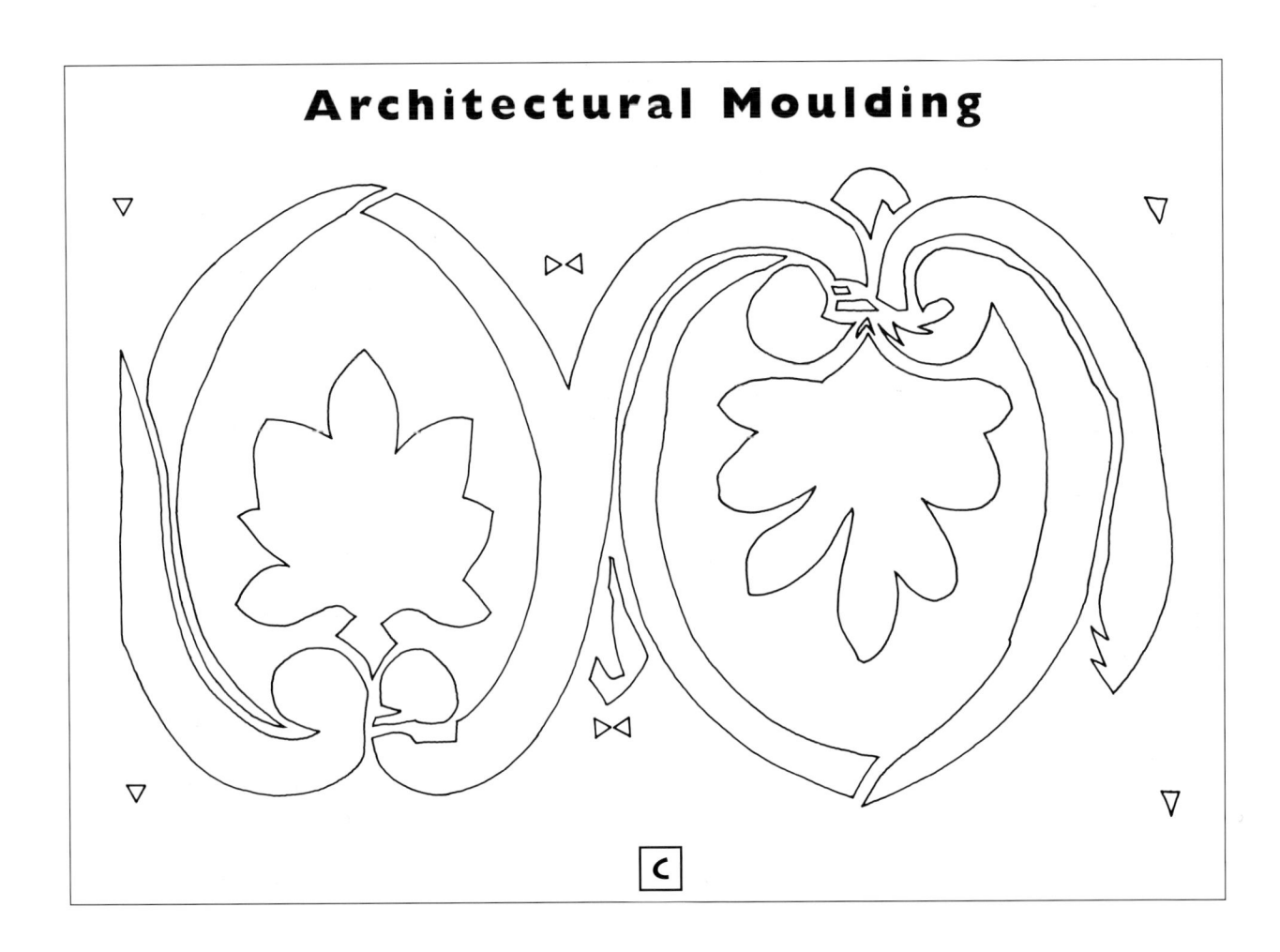

C

# SOURCES

## SUPPLIES AND TOOLS

**Allied Reprographics**
2nd Floor
39 Liverpool Street
Sydney NSW 2000
Tel: (02) 206 6000

**Art Basics**
916 Victoria Road
West Ryde NSW 2114
Tel: (02) 807 2359

**Artiscare (Aust) Pty Ltd**
93 York Street
Sydney NSW 2000
Tel: (02) 299 4151

101 York Street
South Melbourne VIC 3205
Tel: (03) 699 6188

65 Mary Street
Brisbane QLD 4000
Tel: (07) 210 0566

**Deans Art**
21 Atchison Street
St. Leonards
Sydney NSW 2065
Tel: (02) 439 4944

**Janet's Art Supplies**
145 Victoria Avenue
Chatswood NSW 2067
Tel: (02) 4177 8572

**Jasco Pty Ltd**
118-122 Bowden Street
Meadowbrook NSW 2114
Tel: (02) 807 1555

**Oxford Art Supplies**
221 Oxford Street
Darlinghurst NSW 2010
Tel: (02) 360 4066

**Art Stretchers Company**
104 John Street
Brunswick East VIC 3057
Tel: (03) 387 9799

## HOUSE PAINT, GLAZE AND VARNISH MANUFACTURERS

**Croda Paints**
183 Prospect Highway
Seven Hills NSW 2147
Tel: (02) 674 1122

42-48 Cochrane Road
Moorabbin VIC 3189
Tel: (03) 553 1844

**Dulux Australia**
15 Gow Street
Padstow NSW 2211
Tel: (02) 794 9777

McNaughton Street
Clayton VIC 3168
Tel: (03) 542 5678

21-23 Tikalara Street
Regency Park SA 5942
Tel: (08) 348 4100

393 Bass Highway
Launceston TAS 7250
Tel: (002) 44 4555

Murphy Street
O'Connor WA 6163
Tel: (09) 314 4666

1477 Ipswich Road
Rocklea QLD 4106
Tel: (07) 767 8500

**Hodgson's Dye Agencies Pty Ltd**
56 Bay Street
Broadway NSW 2007
Tel: (02) 211 4633

**Maxwell Chemicals**
19 Hale Street
Botany NSW 2019
Tel: (02) 316 6444

**Pascol Paints Australia Pty Ltd**
9-17 Burn Street
Botany NSW 2019
Tel: (02) 666 4311

**Sikkens Wood Finishes**
184-186 Campbell Street
Surry Hills NSW 2010
Tel: (02) 360 4500

**Taubmans Pty Ltd**
7 Birmingham Avenue
Villawood NSW 2163
Tel: (02) 794 1234

Cnr City & Ferreas Streets
South Melbourne VIC 3205
Tel: (03) 690 9203

3 Opala Street
Regency Park SA 5010
Tel: (08) 243 1577

170 Hamilton Street
Queens Park WA 6107
Tel: (09) 451 6744

Winnellie Road
Winnellie NT 0820
Tel: (089) 47 1114

115 Hyde Street
Yeronga QLD 4104
Tel: (07) 892 8888

**Cabot's Wood Stains**
1330 Ferntree Gully Road
Scoresby VIC 3179
Tel: (03) 765 2222
Customer Service:
008 011 006

**Evergard Industries**
Cnr Rufus & Duffy Streets
Epping VIC 3076
Tel: (03) 401 2266

## OTHER SOURCES

**Defender Safety Pty Ltd**
1/22 Artisan Road
Seven Hills NSW 2147
Tel: (02) 853 8986

**Edward Keller (Aust) Pty Ltd**
57 Dooly Street
Alexandria NSW 2015
Tel: (02) 317 5655

**Hang-ups Decorator Warehouse**
40 Fairford Road
Padstow NSW 2211
Tel: (02) 790 2352

**Porter Original Lime Wash**
11 Albion Way
Surry Hills NSW 2010
Tel: (02) 698 5322

**Air-Lac Pty Ltd**
5/59 Hudsons Road
Spotswood VIC 3015
Tel: (03) 391 2122

**Leo's Decorators**
119 McKinnon Road
McKinnon VIC 3204
Tel: (03) 578 4465

**Launceston Art Centre Pty Ltd**
69 York Street
Launceston TAS 7250
Tel: (003) 31 5673

**Tasmanian Paints Pty Ltd**
39 Tasma Street
North Hobart TAS 7000
Tel: (002) 34 4788

**Premier Art Supplies**
43 Gilles Street
Adelaide SA 5000
Tel: (08) 212 5922

**Pyramid Paints**
65 Lipson Street
Port Adelaide SA 5015
Tel: (08) 341 1337

**Paint Traders**
228 Scarborough Beach Road
Mount Hawthorn WA 6016
Tel: (09) 444 5744

**Winnellie Paint Centre**
408 Stuart Highway
Winnellie NT 5789
Tel: (089) 84 4655

**Crown Premium Quality Paints**
246 Robinson Road
Geebung QLD 4034
Tel: (07) 265 2000

## FOR FURTHER READING:

***Recipes For Surfaces***
*Decorative Paint Finishes Made Simple* by
Mindy Drucker and
Pierre Finkelstein
Simon & Schuster Australia
1993

***Complete Guide to Wood Finishes***
by Derrick Crump
Simon & Schuster Australia
1992

***Traditional Paints and Finishes***
by Annie Sloan and Kate Gwynn
Simon & Schuster Australia
1993

***Colour in Decoration***
by Kate Gwynn
Frances Lincoln
1991

***Decorating Magic***
by John Sutcliffe
Francis Lincoln
1992

# Index

## A

abrasive paper, 31, 37, 44, 50
accessories, 68, 79, 81, 82-83, 99
    recipes for, 78, 80, 82, 96, 103, 106, 110, 139, 141, 146, 157, 160, 168, 172
    varnishing, 30
acrylic gel retarder, 33
acrylic medium, 27, 32, 62, 69
acrylic paint. See artist's acrylics
acrylic varnish, 32
additive techniques
    defined, 69
    and glaze application, 34, 67
    ragging on, 15, 69, 117-18, 124-25, 139-40, 160-61
    sponging on, 69, 106-9, 121-23, 126-29, 169
artist's acrylics, 25, 45, 60, 61, 69, 164
artist's oils, 28, 32, 45, 60, 62, 63

## B

base-coating, 40
    application, 49, 50-51
    brushes, use of, 49-51
    for crackle glaze, 157
    defined, 69
    of floors, 86, 126-27
    by material of surface, 54-57
    order of painting room, 48
    primers and, 45
    rollers, use of, 35, 49, 50, 67
    using emulsion, 27
    using oil-based paint, 28
beeswax, 32
binder, 25
blending, 69
brick finish, 68, 115, 126-29
British Colonial style, 172
brushes, 36, 37, 55
    in base coat application, 49-51
    cleaning of, 28
    fitch, 35, 88, 91
    flogging, 70, 151
    foam, 93-95, 97, 111, 128, 132
    loading and holding, 53
    for painting furniture, 53

    quality and cost of, 35
    shape of, 35
    size of, 35
    smoothing out, 71
    stencilling brush, 164, 170
    stippling brush, 35, 71, 78-79
    types of, 35
    varnishing brush, 31

## C

cabinetry
    recipes for, 141, 146, 157, 160
    varnishing, 30
canvas, 136
    surface preparation of, 56
cardboard, 96-99
carpet underlay, 136
ceilings, 124-25
    recipes for, 121, 124, 146, 168
    texture finishes, 136
    varnish and, 30
ceramic surfaces, preparation of, 57
chair rail, 30, 50-51, 130
chalklines, 52, 53
cheesecloth, 37, 62, 69, 132
cheeseclothing, 174-75
cleaning, 40, 43, 54-57, 66
cloth distressing, 69, 70
    cheeseclothing, 174-75
    ragging off, 141-47
    ragging on, 117-18, 124-25, 139-40, 160-61
    rag-rolling, 33
cloudy sky finish, 116, 124-25
colours, 13-15, 17-18, 22-23
    basics of colour theory, 18-23
    brights, 15
    characteristics of, 15, 20
    choosing, 18, 49, 60
    colour wheel, 19
    effects of, 22-23
    jewel tones, 15, 20, 22, 146
    mixing of, 20, 49
    moods and, 21
    neutrals, 14, 20
    pastels, 14
    questions for planning stage, 22-23

    schemes, classic, 20
    schemes, creating, 21-23
    schemes, monochromatic, 13, 20
    temperature of, 21-23
    testing of, 66
    transforming space with, 22-23
columns, recipes for, 92, 103, 106, 110
combing, 69, 70
    graining combs, 36, 52, 130-33
composition, 69, 139
coral, 15
corduroy, 34, 37, 136, 139-43
costs, 34-35, 39-40, 151
cotton swab, 68
counting, 130
crackle glazing, 28, 69, 159. See also glazes
craft knife, 36, 128, 163
credit card, 68
criss-crossing, 49, 69, 88, 104, 128, 146
cutting, 69

## D

dabbing, 69
decorative painting
    defined, 12
    uses and value, 12-13
découpage, 30, 69, 155, 156
    recipe for, 160-63
doors
    base-coating of, 49, 50-51
    preparation chart, 54
    varnishing, 30
dragging, 40, 69, 96-97, 98-99, 110, 111-13
dry brushing, 69, 80, 83
dryers, 29, 33, 70
dusty rose, 14

## E

eclecticism, 13
eggshell paint, 28
emerald, 15
emulsion, 25, 27, 70. See also paints
English Cottage style, 15

English hunting-lodge style, 15
ethnic style, 13, 135

## F

fabrics, surface preparation of, 56
face masks, 33, 34, 36, 43, 45
fade-away, 70
fantasy colours, 70, 87, 92, 97, 101, 106, 127
feather duster, 34, 37
feather-duster finish, 15, 18, 137-38
feathering out, 107-9
feathers, 34, 37, 103-5, 107
filler, 40, 46-47, 54-57
filling, 40, 46-47, 54-57
filling knife, 43, 46-48
fireplace mantels, 103, 106
flatting oil, 62
flogging, 29, 70, 151, 152-53, 172
floors, 26
    base-coating of, 50-51, 86, 126
    brick finishes, 126-29
    glazes for, 29
    preparation for painting, 86, 126
    recipes for, 87, 90, 92, 103, 106, 126, 166
    texture finishes, 136
    varnishing, 30, 86, 126
freehand painting, 32, 86, 88, 90-91
fresco finish, 14, 70, 115, 117-18
furniture
    filling of, 46
    painting of, 53
    preparation of surfaces, 54, 156
    primers for, 44
    recipes for, 78, 80, 82, 103, 106, 110, 130, 141, 146, 157, 160, 166, 168, 172
    skim-coating of, 47
    stripping of, 42-43
    texture finishes, 136
    varnishing, 30, 32

## G

gesso acrylic primer, 56
gilding, 30
glass, surface preparation of, 57

glazes
    application of, 67, 71
    colours, choosing, 49
    with corduroy ragging off, 141-43
    with corduroy ragging on, 139-40
    crackle, 28, 37, 53, 69, 155, 156
        recipe for, 157-59
    defined, 12, 70
    distressing, 34
    for flagstone finish, 88
    for flogging, 151
    for floors, 29, 86, 87
    for fresco finish, 117-18
    for leather finish, 119-20
    making, 29
    manufacturers of, 183-84
    in marbling, 103-5, 103-13
    mixing of, 61-62, 63
    for moiré finish, 130-33
    oil-based, 28-29, 62-63, 117, 119, 141, 151
    with plastic wrap ragging off, 144-45
    premixed, 29
    salvaging, 29
    for stucco finish, 121-23
    suitability to purpose, 29
    testing of, 66
    thinning, 28
    tools for, 34
    waterbased, 27-28
global style, 13, 14, 135, 172
glossary of terms, 69-71
gloves, 34, 36, 43
goggles, 34
gold leaf paint, 82-83, 104
graining, 12, 130, 132-33. See also wood graining

## H

heat gun, 42
hue, 15, 17, 20, 21-23

## I

inlay, 70
intensity, 13-14, 15, 20

## L

lace netting, 136
laminates, surface preparation of, 56
leather finish, 14, 116, 119-20
lemon, 15
leopard skin finish, 29, 151-53
lime, 15
linseed oil, 29, 33, 62

## M

manufacturers listing, 183-84
marbling, 12, 69, 70, 71, 101-13
    basics, 101-2
    blue marbling, 15, 106-9
    defined, 70
    practising, 102, 110
    recipes, 103, 106, 110
    red marbling, 103-5
    sedimentary style, 14, 110-13
    skim-coating, 47
    and varnishing, 30, 32
    veining, 102
    of wall panels, 52
masking, 68, 80-81, 92-95, 119, 126-29, 130, 161, 164, 166, 175
metal finishes, 75-83
    recipes for, 78, 80, 82
    rusted metal, 71, 82-83
    surface preparation of, 57
    varnish and, 30
    verdigris, 78-81
metal primers, 45
metallic paints, 30, 78
moiré finish, 18, 68, 69, 116, 130-33
    defined, 70
    recipe for, 130
    skim-coating, 47
moulding. See woodwork and moulding

## N

natural flow, 70
1950s style, 172

## O

oil varnish, 32
oil-based paint. See paints

186     INDEX

## P

paint pad, 36, 99, 104, 109, 113, 148-49
paints. See also glazes
  amount needed, 32
  base-coating. See base-coating
  choosing a system, 27
  combining water- and oil-based paints, 27
  drying times, 26, 31, 33, 45, 67
  elements of, 25
  emulsion paint. See also water-based paint
  for floors, 86
  glazes. See glazes
  gold leaf paint, 82-83, 104
  gold paint, 30
  labels, reading, 29, 32
  manufacturers of, 183-84
  metallic paint, 30, 78
  mixing of, 49, 59-63, 87
    base coating, 60-61
    glazes, 29
    metallic paints, 30
    premixed vs. scratch approaches, 60
    stirrers for, 35
  oil-based paint, 25, 27, 28, 70
    advantages of, 26
    artist's oils, 28, 32, 45, 60, 62, 63
    dangers of, 26, 34
    drying time, 33
    eggshell paint, 78
    for furniture, 156
    glazes, 61
    system, 28-29
    thinning, 28, 49
    tints, 60
  primers, 44-45
  safety measures in painting, 34
  spray paint, 172
  stencilling, 164
  testing of, 66
  water-based paint, 25
    acrylic gel retarder, 33
    acrylic medium, 27, 32, 62, 69
    advantages of, 26
    artist's acrylics, 25, 60, 61, 69, 164
    base coat, 49
    cleaning, 28
    drying time, 33, 49

    emulsion, 25, 27, 70, 164
    system, 27-28
    thinning, 28, 49
    tints, 60
pale violet, 14
palette, 70, 177
  paper plates as, 34, 36
paper, surface preparation of, 56
papier mâché, surface preparation of, 57
periwinkle, 15
pigment, defined, 25, 70
plaster, 46
plastic bags, 146-47
plastic sheeting, 88, 119
plastic wrap, 136, 144-45
plastics, surface preparation of, 56
polyurethane varnish, 32
Pompeii style, 14
preparation of surfaces, 39-49, 66, 80. See also specific surfaces and techniques
  chart for, 54-57
  découpage, 160-61
  importance of, 39, 156
  tools for, 35
primers and priming, 27, 40, 46, 61, 80. See also shellac
  basics, 44-45
  defined, 70
  floors, 86
  skimcoating and, 47
  surface preparation, 54-57
  tools for, 35
printing, 12, 92, 106. See also specific techniques
pulling, 124-25

## R

ragging, 12, 136
  cheeseclothing, 174-75
  ragging off, 69
    with corduroy, 141, 142-43
    with plastic bags, 146-47
    with plastic wrap, 144-45
  ragging on, 69, 117, 118, 124-25, 160-61
    with corduroy, 15, 139, 140
  rag-rolling, and drying times, 33
  surface preparation for, 40
resins, surface preparation of, 56
rollers, 35, 36
  in base coat application, 49-51
  disposable, 45
  loading and holding, 53
ruby, 15

## S

sacking, 136
safety measures, 34
  with heat gun, 42
  with primers, 45
  with solvents, 56
  with spray paint, 78, 173
  with strippers, 43
sage green, 14
salmon, 15
sample boards, 49, 62, 71
  defined, 66
  experimenting with, 31, 61, 116, 137-38
sanding, 31, 40, 46, 47, 80
  basics, 44
  for crackle glaze, 157
  in découpage, 163
  floors, 50-51, 86
  safety measures, 34
  surface preparation, 54-57
Santa Fe style, 14, 110
sapphire, 15
scrapers, 34, 42, 43, 46
scraping, 43
shade, 20
shellac, 34, 45, 46, 54-56, 61, 71
silver foil, 37, 107, 109
sisal, 136
skim-coating, 40, 47, 48, 54-57
small surfaces, 155-57
smoothing out, 71
solvents, 28-29, 34, 43, 49, 69
spattering, 12, 71, 113
  in four colours, 148, 149-50
sponges, 36-37
  household sponges, 37, 106
  sea sponges, 34, 36, 86, 91, 106, 121-23, 128-29, 169
sponging, 12, 71
  sponging on, 69
    brick finish, 126-27, 128-29
    marble finishes, 106, 107-9
    metal finishes, 80-81
    stone finishes, 91, 92, 93-95
    stucco finish, 121-23, 169
spraying paint, 160
stencil cutter, 36, 164

stencilling, 12, 80, 155
   from acetate, 165, 169, 172, 174
   architectural moulding design, 174-77, 181-82
   basics, 164-65
   from cardboard, 165, 166
   defined, 71
   grape-leaf motif, 116, 168-71, 179
   leopard skin design, 172-73, 180
   multi- vs. singlecolour, 164
   recipes, 165, 166, 168, 172, 174
   registration marks, 164, 172, 173, 175, 177
   repairing stencils, 164, 174-75
   tile design, 14, 166-67, 178
stencilling spray adhesive, 36
stippling, 35, 71, 78-79, 148
stirrers, 35, 36
stone finishes, 14, 85-99. See also brick finish; marbling
   flagstone, 68, 71, 86-89
   granite, 68, 70, 86, 92-95
   malachite, 68, 70, 96-99
   recipes, 87, 90, 92, 96
   stone-work, 86, 90-91, 121
   varnishing and, 30
stripping and strippers, 40
   floors, 42-43, 86
   for spattering, 148-50
   wallpaper, 40, 43
stucco finish, 14, 71, 121-23
subtractive techniques
   defined, 71
   and emulsion, 27
   and glaze application, 67
   with newsprint, 90-91
   with plastic sheeting, 88-89, 119-20
   ragging off, 69, 141-43, 144-47
   tools for, 34
   working in pairs, 66
supplier listings
   miscellaneous supplies, 184
   paint, glaze, and varnish manufacturers, 183-84
   tools and supplies, 183

## T

tacky rag, 46, 157, 161
tape, 36, 68. See also masking
terebine dryer, 29, 33, 70

texture, 13, 86, 90, 135-36
   defined, 71
thinners, 25, 71
tints, 20, 60
tone, 20
tools, 34-35, 36-37
   brushes. See brushes
   cheesecloth. See cheesecloth
   combs, 52, 130-33
   disposable, 34
   feather duster, 34, 37
   household alternatives, 34
   knives, 36
      craft, 128, 163
      filling, 43, 46-48
   preparation tools, 35
   sandpaper, 31, 37, 44, 56
   scrapers, 34, 42, 43, 46
   sponges. See sponges
   suppliers, list of, 183
   tacky rag, 46, 157, 161
   tape, 68
trompe l'oeil, 69
turpentine, 34, 62

## U

universal stainers, 28, 49, 60, 62, 63, 71

## V

vacuuming, 34
value, 20
varnishes, 30-32
   for brick finish, 126-29
   brushes for, 31
   for crackle glaze, 159
   for découpage, 160-63
   defined, 30, 71
   for floors, 86, 87, 89
   for furniture, 156
   manufacturers of, 183-84
   in marbling, 103-5, 105, 106, 109, 110, 113
   removing, 42
   in stone finishes, 92
   for tile stencil, 166
   types of, 32
   yellowing of, 32-32
veining, 32, 70, 71, 102, 171. See also marbling

verdigris
   bronze, 80-81
   copper, 78-79
   defined, 71
   varnish and, 30, 80
Victorian style, 14

## W

wallcoverings, stripping of, 40, 43
walls. See also specific techniques
   base-coating application on, 49-51
   cleaning of, 46
   dividing into panels, 52
   filling of, 46
   fireplace, recipes for, 87, 90
   glazing, 67
   imperfections in, 30, 43, 47
   panelling, recipes for, 92, 103, 106, 110, 137, 141, 146, 166, 168, 172
   preparation chart, 54-55
   recipes for, 110, 117, 119, 121, 126, 130, 137, 141, 144, 146, 148, 151, 166, 168, 172
   skim-coating of, 47-48
   varnish and, 30
water-based paint. See paints
white spirit, 25, 28, 29, 32, 49, 62, 63
wood graining, 26, 52, 69. See also moiré finish
   combs, use of, 70
woodwork and moulding, 26
   base-coating of, 50-51
   marbling of, 52
   preparation chart, 54
   recipes for, 78, 80, 82, 106, 157, 174
   stripping of, 42-43
   techniques for, 155
   varnishing, 30
working dry, 67, 71
working in pairs, 66, 67, 88, 119-20, 151
   with chalklines, 53
   dragging, 70, 110
   graining, 130-33
   ragging off, 141, 146
working wet, 67, 71, 82-83, 87, 88, 125, 132, 152

# RECIPES FOR SURFACES
## Decorative Paint Finishes Made Simple
Mindy Drucker and Pierre Finkelstein
0 7318 0156 3

The forerunner to *More Recipes for Surfaces*, *Recipes for Surfaces* is a handy guide that enables you to master decorative painting techniques for walls, floors, ceilings, and furniture as simply as you would use a cookbook—just follow the recipes. It will show you how to create a variety of exciting surface effects for your entire home using popular basic methods including sponging, ragging, stippling, colour washing, splattering, dragging, stencilling, marbling, and wood graining.

*Recipes for Surfaces* is organised for practical use, with clear and concise explanations, and step-by-step full-colour illustrations. It includes background and specific information on colour, paint and preparation, including advice on how to prepare surfaces, what tools to use and how to store paints.

*Recipes for Surfaces* gives you the confidence and ability to create the painted interior that's right for you.

# TRADITIONAL PAINTS AND FINISHES

## Annie Sloan and Kate Gwynn

0 7318 0317 5

Fashion in decoration is always moving on, and the trend today is towards a rediscovery of traditional paints and paint effects.

*Traditional Paints and Finishes* is a comprehensive guide for the novice and the experienced painter which reveals the classic techniques used by house painters, furniture painters, artists, and restorers. It provides step-by-step instruction in the traditional skills and materials used in wall coating, découpage, limewashing, and glue painting, as well as more complex techniques for fresco, decorating with bronze powders, oil-gilding, and lacquering.

In addition, it provides information on the paints that are available today, and offers detailed instructions for making paints from natural pigments and other basic ingredients.

*Traditional Paints and Finishes* is an important reference for everyone interested in the art of home decorating.

# THE COMPLETE GUIDE TO WOOD FINISHES

How to Apply Stains, Polishes, and Paint Finishes

**DERRICK CRUMP**

CONSULTANT: RONNIE RUSTON

0 7318 0411 2

With over 250 specially commissioned colour photographs, *The Complete Guide to Wood Finishes* is a step-by-step practical guide to a whole range of finishes suitable for use with wood.

The book covers preparation (from stripping to treating stains and dents), and includes finishes suitable for new and restoration work on furniture, floors—indeed, anything made of wood.

*The Complete Guide to Wood Finishes* is a must for every home decorator.